MY WALK PAST HELL
Volume III

Stories of Survival and Overcoming Domestic Violence

DR. YOLANDA J. HENDERSON
VISIONARY AUTHOR

For more information to obtain rights contact or request interview:

Dr. Yolanda J. Henderson
Email: Yolanda@yjempowers.com
Website: www.yolandajhenderson.com
ISBN: 979-8-9881455-1-6
First Printing, January 2024

O LORD, you hear the desire of the afflicted; you will strengthen their heart; you will incline your ear to do justice to the fatherless and the oppressed, so that man who is of the earth may strike terror no more.
Psalm 10:17-18

TABLE OF CONTENTS

DEDICATION

This book is dedicated to all those who have suffered from domestic abuse. To the survivors who have found the courage to leave and rebuild their lives, you are so brave and we stand with you. To those still trapped in abusive relationships, know that you are not alone and there is help available. May you find the strength to break free.

To the victims who lost their lives at the hands of those who were supposed to love them, you will never be forgotten. Your light continues to shine and your memory gives others the power to speak out.

We also pray for the abusers. May they come to understand the harm they have caused and find a better way forward, one of empathy, compassion, and respect for all people. We pray they get the help they need to change their destructive ways.

Though the road is long, we believe in a future free of domestic violence, where healthy, loving relationships reign. There is still much work to be done, but together we can get there. May we join hands, speak out, and bring real change. The time is now!

MESSAGE FROM
THE VISIONAY

Dr. Yolanda J. Henderson

Dear Reader,

The stories you are about to read represent the voices of courageous women who have survived unimaginable pain and trauma from domestic violence abuse. Their stories may be difficult to hear, but it is vital that we listen. For far too long, these women's voices have been silenced and their experiences marginalized.

By sharing their stories, these brave women are shedding light on the horrific reality of domestic abuse that takes place behind closed doors. Their stories give a face and a voice to this global epidemic. They are speaking up not just for themselves, but for the countless other women still trapped in the darkness of abuse.

It is my hope that by engaging with these stories you will come away with greater awareness, empathy and understanding of domestic violence. Perhaps it will open your eyes to the subtle signs of abuse in your own community. You may feel inspired to speak up or lend a hand to someone who is hurting. Or you may gain new appreciation for the strength of the human spirit that allows women to survive and thrive after abuse.

Most importantly, I hope these stories empower you to be part of the solution. There is still so much work to be done to support victims, hold abusers accountable and end the cycle of violence. It starts by truly listening to, believing in and embracing survivors. That is what I aim to do by sharing these stories. May they inspire us all to advocate for justice, healing and positive change.

In solidarity,

Dr. Yolanda J. Henderson

THE DAY
I DECIDED TO LEAVE

Dr. Yolanda J. Henderson

I know many of you have read books and watched television shows and movies depicting stories of domestic violence. Some of those stories have a happy ending and some do not. As you sit and watch, I'm sure you often ask, "Why didn't she leave?" Or you'd say, "I would never allow that to happen to me." But be honest with yourselves, you never really know how you would react in a situation until it happens to you. Don't find fault in the victim, instead put yourself in her shoes and understand her struggle and the things that she must be going through. Why is she staying? Why won't she fight back? Why isn't she telling someone what is happening to her? When is she going to leave? How can she love someone who is beating her? She is just crazy for allowing him to beat her.

We all face fears, obstacles, and difficulties in our lives. And we all reach that pivotal point in our struggle when we must decide to overcome it. Are we going to allow ourselves to drown in these experiences? Or are we going to pick up the pieces, learn from them, move forward, and allow that pain to empower us? There's power in pain. I'm living proof of it. We are all living proof of this. So, here's my story…

The day I decided to leave was the day I took my first step toward answering those questions for myself. It was the day I decided I was no longer going to allow anyone to define who I was or how I was going to live my life. While this is a decision many people will have to make in their lifetimes, it's an especially difficult one for those men and women crippled in the throes of domestic violence. My story is hard to tell, as it's one that represents the more than 10 million victims throughout the United States who suffer in silence every year. That's an average of twenty people who experience intimate partner physical violence every minute.

While serving in the Air Force, I was reassigned to Osan Air Base in Pyeongtaek, South Korea in November of 1997. I made a few friends, and one night we went out on the town to have some fun. While out with the ladies, I met a very charming young man. We talked and had a great conversation, and I learned that he was also in the military, and we were stationed at the same military base. We became friends and soon began dating.

The months just seemed to fly by, and it was time for me to take my mid-tour leave back home to the States. He knew that once I returned from my leave, we would only have a little bit of time left in South Korea to be together, so he tried to convince me not to travel back home. I had already paid for my travel, and I was not willing to budge. There was no way that I was going to lose my money.

As I was preparing to leave, he decided to propose a few days before my flight home, "Will you marry me?"

"I need some time to think about it."

"If you love me, you'll stay here with me."

"You are making it difficult, but I need to go home to see my family. I will have your answer once I get back."

I took my leave and spent thirty days at home with my family. When I returned to South Korea, I said yes. We were married in August of 1998. He received his reassignment orders to Langley Air Force Base in Virginia, and in November, I received my orders and followed him to Virginia.

When we were finally together in Virginia, we rented a townhouse. We settled into our new life and met some friends. I thought things were going well, but within a few months, things began to change. We argued all the time, which would often end with him leaving me at home alone. I began to live my own life by hanging out with my own friends. This, of course, did not sit well with my husband. It was okay for him to stay out all night until the next morning yet wrong for me to do the same. Our fights went from verbal to physical. He did whatever he could to inflict pain on me by grabbing, punching, or slapping. At that moment, I became an abused woman. I would try to lock myself in the bedroom as things began to get worse. After our fights, I was left bruised and in pain.

Divorce crossed my mind, and I thought about it seriously, but in May of 1999, I learned that I was pregnant. The news caused me to stay because I wanted my child to grow up with both parents. For our unborn child, we decided to work on our marriage. The first thing we decided to do was purchase our first home together.

For a little while, things were good and peaceful. Unfortunately, my peace did not last long. The further along I got in my pregnancy, the worse he became. To make matters even worse, he began drinking as well. I remember us arguing and fighting before attending a baby shower we were invited to. This caused me to be emotionally upset, and since I was pregnant, it caused me to become sick to my stomach.

"I'm not feeling well, and I need to stay home."

"No, you're going." Since I was six months pregnant and didn't want to fight anymore, I agreed to go to the baby shower. It was at that moment that I realized I needed to watch what I said and how I said it. I feared the abuse; it wasn't just physical, but it was also mental.

I gave birth in January of 2000 to a beautiful baby girl. For me, nothing else mattered because I was now living to be her mother and protector. My husband did as he pleased, and I really didn't care because our baby was my priority. When our baby girl was four months old, I decided to confront my husband about his absence and lack of care for our daughter. I said some mean and hurtful things, but I was upset. Of course, this led to a fight, and in my attempt to get away from him, I fell down the stairs. I made it to a phone and called 911. The police came, I filed a report, and he was told to leave the home. For days, he called saying he was sorry repeatedly. He promised never to hit me again because he wanted his family back. I was an emotional wreck, and my heart wanted to believe he was sincere. Wanting us to be a family, I allowed him to return to our home.

After being back home for a few days, he was served a letter to appear in court. I accompanied him to court; I didn't want to hurt our family, and I couldn't stand to see him go to jail. I asked the judge to drop the charges, and the judge's response was, "He either gets charged and does his time or he can sign up for anger management courses." Needless to say, he accepted the classes.

In 2001, we were reassigned to Keesler Air Force Base, MS. I was excited to be close to my family. True to form, he became abusive within months of our relocation. I withdrew and became distant from him at this time. I focused on my daughter, my career, and getting promoted to the next military rank. For the first time, I was looking forward to the future for my daughter and me. Also, I was ready to finally file for divorce.

One night in September of 2003, we had another abusive and unbearable incident. He left me with visible bumps and bruises; I couldn't hide them as I had done so many times before. That night, I felt as if I was fighting for my life, while my daughter slept in her room. In an attempt to get away, I ran into our master bedroom and tried to shut the door but couldn't. He grabbed me, threw me on the bed, pinned me down, and spit in my face several times including calling me a "BITCH." He told me I was not going anywhere. My daughter then came into the room screaming at the top of her lungs yelling, "Mommy, Mommy, Mommy!" He stopped when he heard her voice and left the house. He returned later, so I ended up sleeping with my daughter in her room for the rest of the weekend.

My bruises were still visible on Monday morning, and I had to wear make-up for the first time. One of my co-workers noticed, "You are wearing make-up today, and you look different." I, of course, lied and said, "I wanted to try something different." An hour later, I was called into the first sergeant's office. He looked me in my eyes and said, "Yolanda, what's going on?" This was my opportunity to tell someone of the hell I was living, so I decided to tell him everything. Afterward, I ended up at the emergency room for photos to be taken and my husband's leadership was notified. I also had to go through counseling with family advocacy.

Even after all that, I still did not leave. There was one more time of abuse. I can still remember that day like yesterday. My daughter was just three years old. We were at our home and an escalated argument and fight turned deadly when he threw a heavy snow globe at me with such force that had it made contact, it could have killed me. When it didn't, my abuser did what he normally did, fled the scene.

I was on the floor. I was injured badly from the fight, but I wasn't dead. I thanked God at that very moment that my life had been spared. I then looked up and met eyes with my daughter who for the first time had stood witness to the horror I had been living in for years. She was frightened and confused. Emotions that unfortunately, over time, had become normal for me. But the time had come.

I was ready to take both my future and that of my daughter into my own hands. I knew that the next time I encountered my abuser I may not be so lucky. So, while he was away, we made our escape. I scooped up my daughter, and we left our home, taking the first step in saying goodbye to the perilous life we had become accustomed to. At this point, I still wasn't sure what to do, but I knew that I didn't want to stay home. I called a close friend; my husband didn't know where she lived, and I told her about what happened. I told her we needed a place to stay. She said, "You and your baby come stay at my house as long as you need."

The violence I endured had broken my spirit, and I had lost my faith that I would make it through these dark times — but I'd be damned if I was going to impress the same fate onto my daughter. I had to prove to her and to myself that not all hope had been lost. It was waiting for us. I could see it in my mind's eye. I knew I had to make a choice, one that would change our lives forever. And while I knew my decision meant freedom from bondage and a fresh start for us both, it also meant having to face my fears of the unknown. How were we going to make it on our own? How would I support us financially? How would we remain a whole family unit if there was no father figure? Even as I pondered these questions that had trapped me in an abusive relationship, I finally took advantage of the opportunity to set myself totally free from my abuser. One morning, I decided to contact my first sergeant to get the help and resources I needed. I made the decision that neither I nor my daughter would ever return home.

Instead, I received medical care, started counseling, and, along with my daughter, stayed with my friend for a while. I filed for divorce in October 2003, and it was finalized in January 2004. I was finally FREE! All along my journey to becoming free and never going back, I was blessed to have a support network — my dear friend who sheltered us (I could never repay her), my immediate family, and my military family — that protected me throughout the process and helped guide me back to my independence. I'll never say my road to recovery and self-love was easy or that my journey to healing didn't hurt like hell. But for me, ultimately, my saving grace is my daughter.

She was a constant, nagging reminder that I wasn't living my best life as an example for her. I was her role model in a world full of doubt and uncertainty, and God had not asked anyone else but me to fulfill that role for her. And today, I take my role as a mother seriously.

As both a mother and a mentor, I remind my daughter, along with the countless other victims of domestic violence, that when you realize you must love yourself and let go of what no longer serves you, it is the biggest release. And when that release came for me, I suddenly began to clearly see the plans that had been there for me to see all along. The obstacles I overcame and the lessons I learned had put me on my path to my purpose.

The building blocks for my present success as a motivational speaker, author, life coach, entrepreneur, and serving in ministry began many years ago. After surviving my abuser, in 2005, I was led to serve in an advocacy role for sexual assault victims at the military base where I worked. Having been a sexual assault victim myself, I volunteered my time and was instrumental in helping establish the Sexual Assault Prevention and Response (SAPR) Program in the Air Force. I was actively involved with the program until I retired in 2014.

After retirement, I couldn't ignore my desire to continue working with victims of abuse. I was driven to help people, and I couldn't wait to start exercising my humanitarian skills and expertise outside of the confinements of the military. Since that moment, whether through social media, motivational speaking, or my books, my business has been about putting my experience with domestic violence into the world to advocate, educate, and guide fellow survivors through their healing and recovery process. My goal is to empower survivors to recreate a better life for themselves. I also motivate survivors to become focused on their purpose in life and to execute obtainable goals one day at a time.

My message to victims, whether a man or a woman, is simple: You're not alone. Cultural and social change is obtainable when information is made accessible to all who are affected by intimate partner violence. My hope is that victims and survivors will search the internet for information concerning domestic violence. There's an unlimited supply of resources at your disposal.

I offer these helpful safety tips for those who are victims of domestic violence:

1. Have an **escape plan**. Know all the exits in your home, or if in another place, search all exit doors or windows in case you need to utilize them.
2. Create a **safe word or phrase**. This will be a word or phrase only your family, friend, co-worker, etc. will recognize when you are in a violent or emergency situation.
3. Call 911 immediately if you are being abused. Save the phone numbers for the **National Domestic Violence Hotline** 1-800-799-SAFE (7233), a local domestic violence shelter, and someone you can trust to assist you in this situation.
4. Download a safety app.
    a. **DocuSAFE** is a free app that helps survivors collect, store, and share evidence of abuse, such as domestic violence, sexual assault, stalking, online harassment, and dating violence. If survivors choose, the app provides options for sharing the content with law enforcement, attorneys, victim advocates, and other professionals. www.techsafety.org/docusafe
    b. **The SafeNight** app provides support to victims of domestic violence, human trafficking, and sexual assault seeking urgent shelter. www.safenightapp.org
    c. The **Tech Safety App** offers resources for survivors of technology-facilitated stalking or abuse and the advocates who assist them. www.techsafetyapp.org

As a strong believer in the idea that your experiences shape who you are, I stand by my most publicized quotes: "Your setback is a setup for a major comeback," and "Accept the past, focus on the now, impact the future." It's also the reason why I choose to never forget my trials and tribulations as a victim of domestic violence. It is the reason I continue to embrace them and share them with others today.

If it wasn't for the pain those experiences caused me, I may not have ever taken advantage of the power God has bestowed on me and that I use today to continue my fight against domestic violence and to give guidance and encouragement to so many others fighting alongside me.

The day I decided to leave was the day I learned to love myself and fight for myself. I'm a SURVIVOR who's thriving and continues to heal daily. Oh, and guess what? After many years have gone by, in the first quarter of 2023, God blessed me with a loving husband, Frank, who is also my pastor. Now we're doing life, business, and ministry together. #Oneness… Won't God do it!!!

Thank you for taking the time to read my story, and I truly hope it is one that has inspired and encouraged you.

Blessings, Dr. Yolanda J. Henderson- The Empowerment Advocate

Isaiah 61:3
"And provide for those who grieve in Zion- to bestow on them a crown of beauty instead of ashes, the oil of joy instead of mourning, and a garment of praise instead of a spirit of despair. They will be called oaks of righteousness, a planting of the Lord for the display of his splendor."

Dr. Yolanda's Bio

Advocacy is the beating heart of every philanthropist, and exemplifying this principle with utmost dedication is the multifaceted professional, Dr. Yolanda J. Henderson. Born as Yolanda Jones, she hails from the spirited city of New Orleans, Louisiana. Driven by her personal journey as a survivor of domestic violence abuse and sexual assault, she has risen to become an international best-selling author, inspirational speaker, astute business visionary, and the esteemed CEO and founder of YJ Empowerment Solutions LLC.

This visionary enterprise is a comprehensive advocacy program meticulously crafted to empower clients to transcend their past traumas, enabling them to soar to new heights, both in their personal lives and professional endeavors. Fondly known as the "Empowerment Advocate," Dr. Henderson is known for her exceptional ability to resonate with audiences spanning multiple generations, delivering impactful and relatable messages that passionately champion truth, healing, resilience, and personal growth.

In addition to her philanthropic endeavors, Dr. Yolanda J. Henderson is a distinguished retired Air Force veteran.

She also serves as the director of women's ministry at EPIC Fellowship Church in Rocky Mount, North Carolina, where her leadership and guidance have left an indelible mark.

A highly respected figure on both the local and national fronts, Yolanda has been prominently featured in esteemed publications.

One of her most celebrated contributions is the article titled "The Day I Decided to Leave." This powerful testament of survival left such an indelible impression that it was handpicked by the renowned producer and screenwriter, Shonda Rhimes, to be showcased in her online storytelling platform, Shondaland, in 2020.

Furthermore, Dr. Henderson has been honored with the Lifetime Achievement Award, a prestigious recognition bestowed upon her by President Joe Biden and Vice-President Kamala Harris.

Beyond her advocacy work, Dr. Yolanda J. Henderson embodies the roles of a loving wife, mother, and friend, weaving a tapestry of compassion and care in every facet of her life.

Contact and Booking Information
Website: www.yolandajhenderson.com
Social Media: @yjempowers (Facebook, Instagram, Threads)

IT WAS TOO MUCH TO BEAR FOR MY YOUNG EYES

By Brenda Young

A s a parent, I often find myself reflecting on the challenging experiences of my own childhood. These reflections have led me to make a solemn promise to shield my kids from the hardships I endured. From an early age, I had always held the conviction that if I were ever to become a parent, I would spare my children from the negative influences that surrounded me during my formative years.

My journey begins with a stark realization: my upbringing was far from idyllic. I grew up in an environment marred by domestic violence, where the devastating effects of conflicts between my parents left an indelible mark on my young mind. The turbulence within my household cast a dark shadow over my early years, shaping my perception of relationships and setting the stage for the challenges that lay ahead.

As a child, I was a silent witness to the volatile clashes that raged between my parents. The cacophony of raised voices, shattering glass, and piercing screams served as an eerie backdrop to my formative years. These were not the harmonious melodies of a nurturing home but rather discordant notes that left a lasting impression on my impressionable psyche.

The toll of domestic violence extended beyond the physical realm. It severed the bonds of trust and understanding within our family, transforming our home into a battlefield where love and compassion became casualties. As the years passed, the emotional scars deepened, and the chasm between my parents and me widened. I went into survival mode at a young age; fight or flight kicked in.

One of the most insidious aspects of growing up in an environment rife with domestic violence was the culture of silence that shrouded our home. It was an unspoken agreement that we, as a family, would carry our burdens in hushed tones and behind closed doors. Discussing the turmoil that transpired at home was deemed taboo, a transgression of an unspoken code that dictated our family's secrets remain hidden.

As I matured, I began to comprehend the detrimental impact this culture of secrecy had on my mental well-being. The fear of judgment and reprisal silenced my voice, stifling my desire to escape the oppressive environment that had become my daily reality. The weight of these unspoken truths weighed heavily on my shoulders, further isolating me from those who could offer support.

My brother and I, though fortunate not to endure physical violence directly, were exposed to the relentless storm of arguments and fights that ensued between our parents. These traumatic memories still linger, etching themselves into the recesses of our minds. It was during the most heated disputes that we resorted to desperate measures, like stowing away knives in the oven, a feeble attempt to shield ourselves from the traumatic scenes that played out before our young eyes. We had seen our parents fight before where a knife was used, and a suitcase was the shield of protection. To prevent us from seeing it again, we hid the knives often.

The passage of time did little to heal the wounds inflicted by domestic violence. To this day, when I attempt to discuss these painful experiences with my mother, she vehemently denies any wrongdoing. This denial has strained our relationship, making it difficult for me to confront her about her behavior or seek closure. The refusal to acknowledge the past's painful truths only perpetuates the cycle of suffering. The reality of it all is that it's still causing damage because there is a lack of accountability.

Now, as a parent myself, I bear the weight of my past experiences, a mantle I carry with a solemn pledge. I am determined to ensure that my own children are spared the harrowing experiences I endured during my upbringing. It is my unwavering commitment to create an environment in which my husband and I foster open communication with our children, where their thoughts, emotions, and experiences are met with understanding and empathy, not judgment or retribution.

The pivotal question, "Are you okay?" has taken on profound significance in my journey. I am determined to be the person who poses this question to my family, ensuring that they always know that I am here to listen, to support, and to ask if they are okay. This small yet powerful gesture can create a world of difference, guaranteeing that they never endure the isolation I once did. As a child I was too afraid to express to my parents how I felt about what was going on in the house. I was afraid to express how I felt about their divorce and how I felt when my mom and stepdad split up. I will always give our kids the open door to talk to us, no matter how hard the conversation is.

My personal journey, shaped by the painful specter of domestic violence, has deeply influenced my approach to family and relationships. I've come to understand the paramount importance of creating an environment where my loved ones feel safe to express themselves. This safe space is where they can freely share their thoughts, emotions, and experiences without fear.

In adulthood, I've made it a mission to distance myself from toxic relationships and environments, recognizing the signs of potential harm and prioritizing my safety and well-being. My steadfast belief is that no one should ever tolerate physical harm or aggression in a relationship. True love, in its purest form, should never involve inflicting pain upon someone you care about.

As I navigated various relationships, I questioned whether my choices of partners were influenced by my tumultuous upbringing. Witnessing domestic violence as a child left a lasting imprint, reinforcing my commitment to avoiding toxic dynamics. I was determined to break the cycle and build relationships based on peace, respect, and love.

My commitment to healthy relationships hasn't always been easy. Along the way, I faced challenges and heartaches, moments of doubt when I wondered if I was being too selective or idealistic in my quest for a harmonious partnership. But deep down, I knew that compromising on this fundamental principle would be a betrayal of my true self.

Over time, my dedication to peaceful and loving relationships bore fruit, culminating in finding a partner who shared my vision. Together, we built a relationship founded on mutual respect, trust, and open communication. This partnership was a stark contrast to the chaotic and destructive relationships I had witnessed growing up. As I looked back on my journey, I realized that my determination to break free from the cycle of domestic violence had not only shaped my romantic relationships but also permeated every aspect of my life. I became an advocate for healthy relationships, spreading awareness about the insidious nature of domestic violence and the importance of breaking the cycle.

As I continue on my path of healing, I am resolute in my commitment to encouraging others to embark on their own journeys toward well-being. I believe that by sharing our stories, we can offer solace and inspiration to those grappling with similar struggles. Healing is not a solitary endeavor; it's a collective journey of resilience, self-discovery, and empowerment.

My quest for healing has illuminated the profound truth that the past need not define our present or our future. By choosing to heal, we reclaim our power and transform our pain into strength. Healing is a testament to the resilience of the human spirit and the boundless capacity for growth and renewal.

I've come to understand that living peacefully doesn't mean forgetting one's past but rather integrating it into one's journey in a way that empowers and uplifts. It's about embracing our strength and resilience, allowing them to fuel our determination to create a harmonious and fulfilling life.

Now, as a parent with a profound sense of purpose, I view life with greater clarity and empathy. I understand that disagreements between couples need not devolve into fights and arguments. There are healthy ways to address conflicts, and exposing children to toxic situations is detrimental to all involved.

I strongly encourage individuals to seek therapy to confront the lingering effects of their past and break free from their emotional chains. Finding ways to resolve personal issues without involving children is crucial, because kids absorb everything happening around them.

I have become a youth mentor and a school resource officer, acting as a compassionate listener for children who lack support. My life's purpose is to assist those who have experienced circumstances similar to mine, reassuring them that seeking counseling is not only acceptable but necessary to prevent past traumas from impeding their future.

No child should bear witness to the things I endured growing up, and no adult should shoulder responsibility for the events witnessed during their childhood. IT'S NOT YOUR FAULT. The saving grace for me was finding a way out and realizing that the actions I observed in my childhood had nothing to do with me. I should never feel guilty for desiring a life free from dangerous behaviors.

I will continue to raise my voice against domestic violence and advocate for the protection of children from childhood trauma. I want to inspire others to use their past experiences to uplift and encourage not only themselves but also those around them. Each person possesses a voice, and I firmly believe that God saved them for a reason. They have a purpose in this life. It is perfectly acceptable to distance themselves from toxic environments, even if it means separating from their parents for their own safety and peace of mind. Everyone deserves happiness and good health.

It's alright to speak out about your experiences without fearing anyone's judgment. Love should never bring harm. You are stronger than you realize and braver than you think. Embrace a life filled with purpose and positivity. Surround yourself with uplifting influences while intentionally distancing yourself from distractions and negativity, even if it means separating from the family you grew up with. Understand that some individuals will never acknowledge their own responsibility for their actions, persistently dismissing your perspective as inaccurate.

Nobody can dictate how you experienced something. Your story is uniquely yours, and you possess the power to use it as inspiration for others to transform their lives. Find solace in the knowledge that you are not alone in your journey. Share your experiences with those who can benefit from your wisdom and motivate them to bring about positive change in their own lives. Embrace the opportunity to be a catalyst for transformation and growth. Keep moving forward with confidence, knowing that your story has the potential to ignite a spark of hope in someone else's heart.

My life's journey has been marked by a relentless quest for healing, a voyage prompted by the haunting specters of my childhood traumas. For too long, I found myself unwittingly reliving those painful situations, but as I stand at this juncture in life, I am resolute in my decision not to remain trapped in that past any longer. Healing has become my beacon, guiding me toward a brighter and more peaceful future.

One of the profound lessons I've gleaned from my own arduous journey is the importance of encouraging others to embark on their paths to healing. Trauma can leave us shackled by hurt and anger, but I firmly believe that we all possess the capacity to release those burdens and find solace. It is a journey that may be challenging, but the destination is worth every effort.

One of the most agonizing decisions I've had to make in my pursuit of healing has been to distance myself from one or both of my parents due to their actions. It is a decision that has never been easy, laden with a complex mix of emotions, including sadness, guilt, and even anger. However, I've come to understand that this necessary step was ultimately taken for the preservation of my own mental health.

To have parents from whom one must estrange themselves is a heavy burden to bear. Society often emphasizes the importance of family bonds, and the decision to break those bonds can be fraught with judgment and societal pressure. Yet, I knew that to heal, I had to prioritize my own well-being. Sometimes, the most courageous act of self-love is choosing to protect one's own mental health, even if it means creating distance from those who should have been a source of love and support.

Children are incredibly perceptive beings, absorbing the world around them like sponges. Their experiences and observations shape their understanding of the world and significantly influence their behavior and emotional well-being. It is essential to recognize the profound impact that the environment and adult behavior can have on a child's development. In this essay, we will explore how children are affected by the presence of constant conflict and how the presence of love and encouragement can shape their growth. Moreover, we will emphasize the critical importance of shielding children from adult disagreements to preserve their innocence.

Drawing from my personal experiences, my journey to adulthood was marked by considerable challenges, primarily because I had to acquire crucial life lessons independently. Regrettably, my upbringing left significant gaps in my development, as my parents were entrenched in a continuous cycle of discord and argumentation. Regrettably, my recollections of my biological father and my mother are devoid of any positive moments. During the nine years that my biological father was a presence in my life, no memorable instances stand out. The tumultuous relationship he shared with my mother created a chasm that kept him distant from my brother and me. Numerous years passed before we reestablished communication, and this reunion occurred under somber circumstances at my brother's funeral.

Tragically, following my brother's demise, my mother's consumption of alcohol escalated, casting a shadow over our relationship. I observed my mother inadvertently undermine her connection with my stepfather in the aftermath of my brother's passing. Over the course of their thirteen-year relationship, we bore witness to recurring instances of domestic violence. I am firmly convinced that a significant portion of these issues stemmed from my mother's escalating alcohol consumption.

The absence of positive memories associated with my parents, particularly my biological father, cast a shadow over my formative years. The persistent discord between my parents overshadowed any potential moments of joy or nurturing experiences. This dearth of positive parental interactions left me without a foundation upon which to build a healthy understanding of relationships, communication, and conflict resolution.

Domestic violence overshadowed everything positive that was going on in life for my brother and me. I always prayed for God to give me the strength to be the best person that I could be because I never wanted to have a life like the one I grew up in. It is so important for me to be the best bonus mother I can be for my kids. I can't physically have children, but I can love on my bonus kids as much as the Lord allows me. Being the best example for our four children is what brings me joy. Having a healthy environment for them when they are in our care is the most important factor for my husband and me.

It's important for us to teach our children that putting their hands on someone that they say they love is not okay. My advice to them is that if they ever find themselves in the position where they have to put their hands on their significant other, they are to leave. Be the responsible people that we taught them to be. Life will get hard, and relationships will get challenging, but if it is detrimental to their health, LEAVE.

Prayer and therapy have always been my answer. I found a way to cope and come to peace with my past. I thank God for healing. God has given me so many answers in life and has blessed me with the people who have helped me reach this part of my journey. As hard as it was for me to write about this portion of my life, it was necessary for others to learn that domestic violence affects children more than people see and think. In life, we have to be mindful of what we surround our children with.

Brenda's Bio

Brenda Young is a multi-talented leader, business management graduate, master life coach, bestselling author, youth mentor, Navy veteran, and dedicated school resource officer/police officer.

With a diverse range of skills and experiences, Brenda embodies inspiration, leadership, and service. Her bestselling books, coupled with her expertise as a master life coach, have empowered countless individuals to unlock their full potential.

As a dedicated youth mentor, Brenda uplifts and guides young individuals, helping them navigate life's challenges with confidence. With a background as a Navy veteran, she brings a deep sense of discipline, dedication, and resilience to her work. Brenda's commitment to education is reflected in her bachelor's degree in business management.

She prioritizes community safety and fosters positive relationships, making her a cherished member of her local community, known for her compassion and genuine concern for others. Brenda Young is a true leader.

Contact and Booking Information
Website: www.iambrendayoung.com
Email: brendayoung@byoungenterprisesllc.com

THE "BEAST" RECOGNIZES THE BEAUTY IN ASHES

Geneva D. Ashley

If the precious stone called a diamond could talk, it would have quite a story to tell. It would say that the journey to brilliance and shine was far from easy. It would say that there was a time it was deeply embedded in the deepest confines of the earth, and when it was finally ripped from its most familiar place, its appearance was one that was not the most appealing to the eyes of many that beheld it.

Then it would fervently speak to the rigor of its transformation from the rough exterior and stony gray complexion to clarity and brilliance. There were times that this extremely valuable stone had to undergo a process that required it to endure over

700,000 pounds of pressure and over 2,000 degrees of heated fire until the original chemical element was crystalized. And at times, it felt as though the pressure and heat both were far too much to bear. Then it would let you in on an intimate detail, the fact that the pressure and heat wasn't applied once or twice but several times until it reached the point of purification and brilliance to continue its journey of being molded and shaped for its creator's use.

When the average person thinks of the diamond gem, immediately what comes to mind is a clear, brilliant stone used to adorn in a multitude of ways. Rarely would one think of what it took to achieve its brilliance. Neither would one think on the fact that the diamond was very valuable before it made it to the state of a fashionable piece of jewelry.

You ARE that *DIAMOND*…

Understand that the diamond analogy is a lot like we are as women. How? Well, I'm glad you asked, because the answer is simply this. The diamond had to endure and travel extensively through pressure, high heat, blunt force, and crushing. Nevertheless, no matter what happened along the way, it never lost its value! Now, in the human sense, it is not right to be crushed, tossed about, and pressured. It may even be downright unfair. Yet it was necessary to be effective and make wiser decisions in life.

After living through traumatic experiences, self-love is a behavior many have to learn all over again, and in some cases, for the very first time. Then cultivation of self-love is an entirely different learned behavior. And guess what? The investment in "self" is essential because you deserve to love you. Then you will be able to teach others how to love you. You will recognize the signs that are unacceptable and unapologetically dismiss the treatment from those that do not respect boundaries you have worked so hard to implement to sustain the peace you desire.

Allow me to share a little about domestic violence and why it's so important to understand how to preserve YOU! When one has lived or is living through domestic violence, it will undoubtedly cause chiseling away of esteem, confidence, and a sense of being, even to the degree that one may feel insignificant and invaluable – not right, yet it's a reality! So, after the mental, emotional, verbal, financial, and sometimes physical abuse (to name a few) has ceased, it often leaves one with tear-stained cheeks, low self-esteem, a sunken feeling of non-existence, and brokenness. One may desire to get out of the situation but simply not know where to turn. Attempting to explain it to others or help it make sense to anyone else is nothing short of a daunting task; therefore, many choose not to bother. After all, it's better to work through it alone, right? NOT at ALL! You're not alone, and you're not the only one living the nightmare.

Once upon a time…

Walking through the warm summer breeze and feeling the wind brush softly against her skin is what she enjoyed doing most. As far back as she could remember, the warm weather was always her favorite, because for some reason it offered a sense of calm, comfort, and quiet from the chaos she had grown accustomed to since home was not always a place of peace and happiness, due to the ever-present elements of dysfunction.

Too often fear filled her heart as the sudden screaming, crashes of things breaking, and arguments rang out. So, with tears in her eyes, she would retreat to small, compact spaces. Small spaces seemed to muffle the noise. Small spaces felt cozy and comfortable, which eventually became her hiding places whenever she felt unsafe or afraid. No one else may have known how she was feeling, but the Lord knew because she could freely tell Him all about it without the concern of being jolted by the plague of violence around her. Her granny often assured her that "Jehovah loved her so much because she was very special, and great things were in store for her."

As time passed, she developed a sensitivity to her surroundings, continuing to "steal away" moments to talk to the Lord. It was during these times that the need to steal away had become so regular that her curiosity about purpose grew. Could life and death be all there was? Only time would tell! You may wonder who "she" is…well, SHE is ME!

What was once considered a coping mechanism used to shield the noise of my surroundings became a sustainability tactic! Yes, what I now know as my "prayer life" had become second nature no matter what was happening around me. And as challenges arose and adversity reared its ugly head, the only thing I knew to do was steal away and talk to God.

The storms of life began to rage and were indiscriminate. I had been raped as a pre-teen by someone an older relative who was caring for me knew, sending me into a tailspin of darkness, but I was much too young to recognize it. Although I tried, it made me nervous to tell anyone what happened to me; therefore, I often battled with severe depression, suicidal thoughts, and constantly ran away from home. Eventually, I became a teen parent and started drinking. Still afraid to tell, I blamed myself for many years for the rape, among other things. I felt guilty for not saying anything to my parents or any other adult. Feeling ashamed, unworthy, and unwanted, I attempted suicide twice, and when each time was unsuccessful, I began to believe that even God didn't want me! But before I go on, please allow me to pause here for a quick moment. This writing is not a tale of woes but a testament of struggle, defeat, brokenness, heartache, and pathological pain that have served as tools and ingredients for obtainable deliverance!

The enemy of our Creator seeks to devour the vessels that have been equipped to fulfill the assignment that can and will only result in the victorious proclamation of the only true and living God!

So, after mentally bashing myself over the rape and attempted molestation, being bullied in school, being self-destructive, and teenage pregnancy, it only took a turn for the worst when I landed in an abusive marriage and experienced homelessness three times resulting in being beaten down emotionally, financially, and broken beyond recognition to myself! I felt as though nothing else was left to go through. Everything inside of me was exhausted, and all I knew was I had hit my lowest but was able to muster up enough strength to talk to the One that always seemed to hear me, even in the times I felt unworthy of even whispering in His direction. Once again, I decided to steal away, and guess what? His response was to send an evangelist who would be persistent enough to labor with me six long years, inviting me to church, praying for me, and encouraging me no matter how many times I turned her down.

She invited me one more time, and that visit opened the door to a turning point in my life that I had been seeking since I was a little girl. I was not raised in a traditional church, and my family had a completely different belief system. I had only heard that Jesus was a "good" man or a "great" teacher. So, when I got to the revival, I saw and heard He was so much more. And that stayed with me, and I literally thought about it for several weeks after.

I couldn't rest until I made peace with a place of complete "surrender" to what was unfamiliar.

After toiling with the ramifications of the abuse, unhealthy interactions, and ultimately an unhealthy marriage atop layers of other issues, I was determined to find the "love language" toward myself. Enough had become enough, and my soul was thirsty to locate this purpose and plan from my Creator because I believed there was more to all I had gone through than what appeared on the surface, even more than what people said or thought. Life couldn't possibly only be filled with pain, horrific circumstances, wicked acts, and evil attacks. There had to be more. So, I embarked wholeheartedly in pursuit of finding the true meaning of personal "purpose."

Trials, trouble, and tumultuous experiences had landed me in areas of my psyche that I would have gladly skipped over if I could have.

What I learned later to be my "prayer life" was the place I ran anytime I felt I was being surrounded by harm or danger. It was the place of refuge that would yield results that would calm the fear and melt away shame. I knew that what the abuse brainwashed me into accepting as truth was a cesspool of fabrication from the pits of hell. And it required me to pull out the "microscope" of introspection and search open-mindedly and humbly as I could for the reasons that I had allowed the betrayal, deception, manipulative mind games, and mishandling of me to go on for so long. I had to honestly review the incidents of the past, though painful, to figure out the solution to move differently to receive a positive outcome.

Why was I so easily led to believe that God hated divorce to the degree that I sat and settled for years accepting the mental, emotional, financial, physical, and spiritual abuse in my own home and in the house of God? What part of this could possibly be acceptable in the sight of my Lord and Savior who spoke through His word that He came "that they may have life, and that they may have it more abundantly" (John 10:10b)?

To some, this Scripture may be something read a multitude of times, yet when I read it, bells, alarms, whistles, and glittery flags sounded off and waved inside of me. See, up to this point, I had experienced pain which became second nature. It was almost strange for anything to go in a favorable direction for me. Even though I had found the Lord, I still seriously needed healing, deliverance, and clear comprehension of His Word as well as the knowledge and wisdom to apply it to my life so that I could begin to see myself the way He saw me.

My family had been fragmented because of conflict of religion, which only isolated me from what could have been an extra layer of protection and visibility. No one would have had a clue about danger lurking not to mention those who lived literally minutes away from me at the time but were so self-absorbed they rarely called let alone stopped by.

I can recall a time that I would give God every moment I could. I would work all day, pick up my children from school, get them fed, and we'd all change and head out to every service we could in order to stay out of the home environment that was so toxic. As I stated, I was exiled from my family due to religious conflict, so I was left completely vulnerable to the devices of the enemy, or *so he thought*. One night I'd gotten home after service and walked into a gun on the abuser's lap. Thank goodness it was late, and the children were already sleep-walking into the house.

He allowed me to place everyone in bed before the rant, agitation, and aggravation began. I remember getting extremely upset and fighting my way into the room where my babies were and locking the door. He broke it, so I could not escape out of it. I barely slept for watching the door and praying to keep us all safe in this one room locked away as my heartbeat profusely and so fast and loud it was as though it was on the outside out of my chest.

At the time, a landline was all we had which he'd confiscated all of the cords to and left me no choice but to wait until he left one day to break free and walk to find the closest police station only to be told there was nothing they could do to help because the gun had not been discharged. With my heart sinking and fear gripping everything within me, it was the first encounter I had with the Lord that caused me to feel a level of supernatural boldness. I walked to my relative's home that lived closest; they were not home, so I waited for them to return and told them what happened. They took me back to the house the next day, and I eventually moved out. This set off an entire new series of events that were used as fear tactics to no avail. Yet one thing I learned through it all was that the Scriptures I'd been ingesting and digesting despite being exiled from my family, isolated and rejected, had come alive within me. I leaned heavily on I Timothy 1:6-7, "Wherefore I put thee in remembrance that thou stir up the gift of God, which is in thee by the putting on of my hands. For God hath not given us the spirit of fear; but of power, and of love, and of a sound mind."

The time had arrived to make better decisions come what may. And the opinions of people were a non-factor. I had to apply the Word for myself and live the life God intended.

I found that I could share my innermost thoughts and deepest secrets without shame and still reap the benefits of a love beyond all knowledge, even though my life was framed in darkness and despair. This newfound liberty afforded me the ability to triumph to a place of peace and contentment I once thought I would never know no matter what others thought, said, approved, or disapproved of. And accepting my newfound journey with Christ cost everything —even my entire family, whose belief system was not the same. Nevertheless, what once burdened my heart with worry and concern of rejection simply no longer mattered and was overshadowed with joy.

Though a very colorful and dark past at times, it is my truth, my story. It is the one that prepared me to become a woman of confidence with a level of boldness that is unique and incomparable, because God loved me enough to teach me how to fall in love with Him, instructing me and guiding me to this unapologetic place of self-love, all the while qualifying me to share with others how to do the same!

I have unapologetically learned to embrace vulnerability and discomfort as part of my makeup as a woman. I learned that it was okay for me NOT to be okay at times. The framework from which I was raised has waxed into a beautiful vessel called and equipped by the masterful hands of a God who is strategic and intentional in all His ways. Though I am imperfect, He is yet perfect. I found that what was designed to destroy me only caused me to transform into the effervescent personality I am today.

As a woman with many gifts, callings, and experiences, who strives to be the kingdom ambassador and change agent in a time when the world is struggling to decipher authenticity from simple identity, I traded ashes for beauty, because I was blessed to receive the "keys" to the kingdom that changed my life!

The likelihood of past hurts and betrayal is what causes one to become guarded and insecure in the establishment of new relationships or allowing ourselves to get too close to anyone. The fear of trusting anyone is ever-present when lessons of life have left us holding our hearts with tears streaming down our faces.

At some time or another, every person on the planet has felt the emotional deficit left by betrayal, deceit, or the lies from a so-called "friend" that flipped to a foe, leaving us facing the void and emptiness of loss. Yes, it has happened to the best and the worst of us. My story was riddled with abuse, but someone else's may be filled with something else. Nevertheless, life goes on, and God restores.

What started as a "safe escape place" for me known as a time to "steal away" was really meant to seize "microcosms" in time for purposes of clarification without interruption. This very well can keep one from "free-falling" into situations that could lead to a "dead-end."

I don't look like the hell that I've walked through. Yet the secret in the sauce is the walk "through," not stopping long enough to look back or dwell on the past although the flaming fire sent to try you may seem close enough to engulf you; you will "come out as pure gold." (Job 23:10) Nothing can override the "plans God has for you!" (Jeremiah 29:11)

In closing, I leave you with this quote:

"The pain of the past is beautiful because the thoughts and plans God has for us illuminates so brightly that the "beast" who set out to destroy you is literally blinded by your light." ~Geneva D. Ashley~

Geneva's Bio

Geneva D. Ashley, formerly Geneva D. Holmes, hails from the northern California Bay Area with roots in Louisiana.

She is the first-born granddaughter to Pastor Henry Holmes, III and Ruth Holmes and is cut from an intricate cloth in ministry. Humble but gifted, Geneva was very shy and introverted, yet her parents noticed she thrived most when in environments that allowed her to help others. As a violinist, writer, and artist, she embraced the multi-faceted assignment she was created to fulfill.

Now, Geneva is a domestic violence VICTOR with a ministry of many folds. As a wife, mom, best-selling author, keynote speaker, life strategist, and an ordained servant leader, in addition to being the co-president of MG Decree LLC alongside her husband, she is an avid philanthropist.

In these roles, she continuously and unapologetically strives to uplift, empower, and encourage women from all walks of life while connecting her heart and hands with the masses as God sees fit employing a judgment free approach!

In 2023, the Lord called Geneva and her husband to launch the WIFE Support LIFE Support Master Class and Annual Brunch experience. This is a two-fold ministry for wives, husbands, and those seeking to prepare for marriage.

A woman of many accomplishments, Geneva remains humbly grounded, stating in her own words: "I'm just "G" without apology, grateful and gifted to be used of God so mightily!" Stay tuned…

Contact and Booking Information
Instagram: SHEisGenevaDAshley
Email: MGDecree@gmail.com

R.I.S.E. OF THE QUEEN PSALM 139:14 "FEARFULLY & WONDERFULLY MADE"

By Mavis A. Creagh

I remember sitting in the passenger seat on a dark road and being told to open my mouth while the barrel of a gun was being shoved in. I wept and thought this is not how my life is supposed to end. Silent tears streamed down my face. He told me to taste the metal, and I sensed him smirking a little bit while I wondered if I would make it back home to my son.

We were coming back from my friend's birthday party. It was a beautiful celebration with live music, dancing, and fun. My spouse at the time sat at the table but something was amiss.

My life did not end that night, and after he pulled the gun out of my mouth, I tried to speak out but did not have the words to express the confusion, frustration, anger, and pain. He laughed it off and shrugged while saying there were no bullets in the gun. Basically, I was told to just get over it. I felt so scared, heartbroken, and devastated. We were just okay, and this craziness happens. He had even mentioned that one of my friends reminded him of his mother who had died recently. I wish I could say that was the worst event that happened while being with my ex or that I left after this occurred, but that is not my story. After that night, we never spoke of what happened again.

That was around year six of our relationship as we lived together in a house that we shared. I thought he would be my husband; he even promised me this for years... but ultimately, that never happened. My son was around three when we met, and at one time, I thought even if he is not always nice to me, at least my son will have a man in his life. I was so wrong to think that, and it almost cost me my life.

I went back to my normal routine, and it, of course, did not get better. There were sporadic incidents for about a year or so, and then the bottom dropped out. That is how I remember it, but there probably are things that I blocked out of my memory. Truthfully, some seasons or years of my life I cannot remember. This has been attributed to severe trauma and in some instances can be linked to symptoms of post-traumatic stress disorder. Even times in my life from before the relationship I am unable to remember. It is like I was and wasn't at the same time. Existing and not alive...A wanderer in my own journey. I am more intentional now about who I allow in my life and try to share with other women and people in general to protect yourself at all costs, even if you must break connections to family, friends, jobs, or partners.

I have learned that there are some people sent to see just how far they can take you into hell. If you are not watchful and vigilant emotionally, spiritually, and mentally, predators will attempt to prey on those who they deem as broken and weak. I hope by sharing my experiences that others are helped and feel confident to know that even though you may be in hell, just escaped hell, or been out of hell for some time, you can always pull yourself up and get out.

That was not the last act of abuse but only the beginning of a list of heinous acts that went on for years. Over time, you begin to break down emotionally, mentally, and no longer have the will to fight for your life. Being in a domestic violence relationship is like a vice grip getting tighter, choking out your voice. You become conditioned to speak but with no authority or power. Even when you talk, it is from a place of reservation because you do not want to upset your partner in fear of retaliation. By sharing, I want to encourage women and even men that your life matters, and the situation does not get better but only worse. Even if there are cycles with signs of affection, concern, and care, it can all shift in a matter of seconds, and it is like playing a game of Russian roulette with a loaded gun. Imagine when that barrel was in my mouth; that is the game that those who stay in abusive relationships are playing.

Some would ask how it could get any worse, but as I wrote this in my notepad first, there were tears from remembering just how horrible it was at times. My life was transformed into a cycle of torture, physical, emotional, verbal, and sexual abuse all with the assertion of control, lies, and manipulation. At times, it felt like psychological warfare.

Closer to what I thought was our separation, he became even more abusive and more agitated with me. I could do nothing right, and it was like he was looking for a reason to react. Repeatedly I was called out of my name with things like "bitch," "cunt," and "whore" while being told that sex was what I was good for. Although this was terrible, due to what I realize was abusive acts even as far back as childhood, I eventually started to believe him. My identity became broken, causing me to be depressed and suicidal. During this time, I relapsed and became dependent on alcohol. There were times when I did not want to drink or smoke, and my ex would strongly encourage and sometimes force me to. One time, I literally thought I was going to have a heart attack, and years later, I found out that I had heart issues. I don't know if it was an issue that I had all along, but I do know repeated stress and trauma can kill you, and abuse can kill you.

I remember sharing some very personal things with my former spouse earlier in our relationship. I thought that he was safe, and I could trust him. This was one of the worst things that I could have done at that time. He used my pain against me, and it eventually felt like I was drinking poison every time he brought it up. With his twisted logic, he tried to force me to do things that I was uncomfortable with. The coercion went from suggestions to acts of retaliation for me not complying. This included rape, sexual aggression, and other acts of violence. As a result of my noncompliance, there would be beatings, threats, and torture.

A very low moment I experienced was having outside people tell me about his advances and manipulation. I felt so degraded and humiliated when it was not only external persons but my ex confirming my fears. Some others even thought this was funny, made hurtful remarks, and laughed at my pain. It felt like he balled up his fist and was trying to crush my soul while slowly extinguishing my will to live. He hated me but did not want to let me go. This is a scary part for women who are in abusive relationships. An act of violence out of rage can turn deadly in a split second.

I was making a mental note of every monumental attack that occurred and decided to just stop counting. One night, I was sleeping in bed and remember being pulled by my hair and thrown onto the bathroom floor. As I lay on the cold floor naked and afraid, once again, my life literally flashed before my eyes. I was unable to speak while being repeatedly pushed back down. Some may ask why did you stay? There is no logical answer for not leaving after so much, but somewhere in my mind, I considered having a family with a man, woman, and children as more important than my happiness and self-worth. This is something that I have worked on so much since leaving, but there are many women who in some way think that the abuse is worth the relationship, position, or title, and that is not true. Your life is more valuable than any relationship! While reflecting, I know the skewed mindset of desiring a "normal" family over safety, love, and happiness is no more than a trick of the enemy and an attack against the creation of the Most High (G_D). Now, I know that my son and I are a whole family. We don't need anyone to make us whole, and our family unit is just as complete even without a spouse.

There were multiple incidents that I have not even fully processed. I just got through them and moved on to the next. This project has been more challenging than I thought because it is like unpacking. Healing is an ongoing process, and anyone who has lived through domestic violence will continuously be on a lifelong journey. It gets better, and you can survive on your own. Even if you must give up everything that you know to save yourself, your mind, body, and soul are worth it. You can always start over!

This was not the first person who abused me, and after much reflection, there was a hidden pattern of abusive relationships. The other situations were not physical and ongoing, but there was a trait of attracting those who did not value and respect me. This is something I am unpacking and working on through my journey. When you are in a better place within yourself, many times, you can recognize these types of people, and even if you do not upfront, you will have the courage to remove yourself once an incident occurs. However, when you are broken emotionally and spiritually, you are more prone to allow others to mistreat you and not stand up for yourself.

Once, when I did try to stand up for myself, my ex told me that he would get me back... for speaking up. When he returned home, I was beaten, and I remember vividly saying repeatedly that I did not deserve this.

Even after almost ten years, my son and I were forced out of the house we shared together. Later, I found out there were other reasons for his persistent push. I was still trying to hold on to the false narrative of what a whole family looked like. Even after moving out, he still would randomly show up to my new apartment, and I would at first cave in. After a while, I decided to really let the situation go and decided to move on with my life. Many don't realize that women are still at risk after leaving an abusive situation. Some men still want access and control even outside of the relationship. My ex would show up at night unexpectedly, ringing the doorbell, and even once began hitting his fist against the door. I can remember putting furniture in front of the door sometimes and laying in the bed frozen in fear. He expected me to pick up where we left off, give access, and start back like before. I know this sounds foolish after everything that happened. Somewhere in the back of my mind, I still wanted to be with him and desired happiness with him. This desperate desire almost cost me my sanity and life.

One morning, I was getting ready after dropping my son off at school, and as I was getting out of the shower, I heard the doorbell ring. At that time, I was really trying to be strong and move forward. It's sad, but during this time, I was not as offended about the abuse as knowing that he wanted to deal with me but no longer wanted to be in a relationship with me. It's crazy now that I truly think about it. When I refused to open the door, I heard the locks turn and my ex let himself inside. I did not know that he had made a key to my apartment without me knowing. I was assaulted on that day. I can remember being hit, and large imprints of his hand were left on my back and body. I told him that I hated him for what happened. I got up feeling alone and hopeless like so many times before. It was like the pain would never end, and I could never free myself from this evil. I can remember him running his hand over my beaten back as if to see what visible damage he had caused. I was dead and alive, breathing and suffocating at the same time. I made him give me back the key and told him that I hated him.

The only thing that I truly remember after that is I was alive. I am so grateful now to be in a different place in my life and know what freedom looks like. It is not an easy process, but I would rather be free than try hopelessly to make someone love me correctly. I have no contact with him, and it was not easy, especially early on. Later, it became more of a cat and mouse game to see if I would lose focus and slip back. Abusers will wait you out but going back can be your last time at life. I am still cautious even after over four years. I am not fearful but remain careful. My guard is not down, and that is what survivors need to understand that time does not make an abuser change. They must do the work within themselves and want to change, and even with this, it can be a difficult task.

Many see the women who get abused but never bother to ask them why they stayed and what caused them to think this was okay to begin with. I started counseling after fully removing myself from the relationship and got the opportunity to intently consider these questions. Healed people who are well do not usually stay in situations that break them down. Those who are repeat abusers usually prey on women who are broken from unresolved issues, hurt, and pain. I have worked to identify my pain even as far back as childhood and continuously work on healing.

One of my missions is to let women know even if you stayed for years, this does not make you less of a woman, even though that is how others may try to make you feel. Sadly, even some women are quick to pass judgement on others who have gone through abusive relationships. They may say things such as it could never be me, she looks so stupid, and, of course, you let him hit you! These statements do not encourage women to leave abusers or speak up. Negative dialogue such as this only supports the abusers' tactics of ridicule, humiliation, and dismantling the self-esteem of survivors.

I have learned a lot about myself during the process. There are residual effects to being in a domestic violence relationship. Every area of your life was altered in some way at one time. You must work at healing, and it does not happen overnight. Like I said before, it is a process!

I used to be ashamed of what I had gone through not just with this relationship but also with others who had betrayed me. Immediately following the relationship, I started intense counseling, and somewhere in my mind, I thought that was enough. Now, I realize that when you go through so much and are hurt so bad that is a lot to unpack. There is nothing wrong with counseling and therapy on a regular basis to support your healing journey. I would highly recommend it for anyone who has experienced any trauma, especially survivors of abuse. .

You can survive domestic violence. Even if you must start ALL over, at least you are alive. If you must sleep on the floor, at least you can sleep in peace. My heart breaks for those who did not make it out of domestic violence alive. Even after leaving, your life can still be in danger. As we speak up, my hope is to bring awareness, support, and resources for women who may be thinking about leaving or who have escaped but need assistance. The more we raise our voices, the greater chance that someone else's life may be saved. If you or someone you know is experiencing any form of domestic violence, know that you are not alone. I thought at one time that this would kill me, I would not be able to leave the person alone, and would not be strong enough to completely walk away. As a person of faith, I know that this is not true, and anything is possible.

Thankful to have come through one of the darkest seasons of my life alive with scars, hurt, and pain, but I made it to the other side and lived... walked through hell with my head held high. But I am deeply saddened, because some unfortunately do not make it out alive. For my life, I am forever grateful.

After leaving and making up my mind to choose my life, there were many areas that needed healing, and still to this day, it is a continuous process.

Recovery is a process, renewal is a process, restoration is a process, and it does not happen overnight.

No matter where you are or what you went through...you are a queen!

You deserve to be happy, treated well, loved, and respected.

No matter what hell you have been through, healing is possible, and "it" did not break you. Therapy, counseling, and faith in the Most High (G_D) have truly gotten me through. There are also support groups, mental health resources, survivor circles, and domestic violence advocacy organizations.

You Matter, You Are Loved, and You Are Not Alone.

You Are Not What They Called You…

Stand Up…And R.I.S.E. Queen!

-

Mavis' Bio

Mavis A. Creagh is an executive director, best-selling author, speaker, consultant, mental health proponent, community champion, women's advocate, entrepreneurial strategist, columnist, and online show host.

She currently serves as the executive director of R3SM, Inc. (Recover, Rebuild, and Restore Southeast MS), a nonprofit founded following Hurricane Katrina that specializes in restoration following disasters. She established Mavis A. Creagh Consulting, LLC, a brand that offers editing, writing, speaking, and business consultation; Mavis On Main, a lifestyle and fashion brand that encourages happiness, wellness, and hope; and We Women Ministries, Inc., a ministry created to empower, enrich, and elevate women from all backgrounds around the globe.

She has an extensive knowledge of recovery following natural disasters with a foundation in revitalization of communities, philanthropy, and economic development. Over the past six years, Mavis provided oversight of thirty-one new constructions, 200 plus repair projects, and approximately 7 million dollars in volunteer labor and donations throughout the state of Mississippi.

Her presentation entitled "Empowering Resilient Communities" was presented at the National VOAD (Volunteer Organizations Active in Disaster) Conference in Baltimore, MD last year. She was elected to serve as a representative on the NVOAD housing committee and housing chair for Mississippi State Conference NAACP.

In addition, she serves on multiple boards including Disaster Leadership Training (National Disaster Mentorship Organization), Mississippi VOAD (Volunteer Organizations Active in Disaster), NAMI Mississippi (National Alliance on Mental Health), and Mississippi Conference of the NAACP. Most recently, she was awarded Top 10 Businesswoman of the Year for 2022 by Mississippi Business Journal and the Amy Lyon Community Service Award by Pine Belt Veterans Task Force in 2023!

Her proudest accomplishment is being the mother to an amazing teenage son, Jordan, a science and math enthusiast, basketball buff, and trained chef.

Contact and Booking Information
Social Media: Mavis A Creagh (Facebook, Instagram, LinkedIn)
Website: www.mavisacreagh.com

NEVER SAW IT COMING

By Lisa Evans

On my way to work, I decided today was the day I was going to leave him. I just cannot take any more abuse. My plan was instead of going to the apartment after work, I would stay out and get home extremely late to upset him. Once he started punching me, I would figure out how to get the police involved, and then they would let me get my stuff, and it would all be over.

I should have known my plan would not work because I could never predict his actions. My part of the plan went into effect, and yes, he started punching me. I broke away this time, went into the bathroom, and called the police for the first time.

Once they arrived, he was calm but angry. The two officers listened to me and then to him. They advised me to stay since they had come by; they felt he would not hit me anymore. So, now my plan was not working, and they did not help me pack my things to get away. Now, I was confused and did not know what to do. So, like a fool, I listened and stayed.

Once the police left the apartment, I was thinking of how I could jump off the balcony and only break a leg since I was only on the second floor. Then I thought if I could just get away, I would run for help. But with the heavy grip on my neck, I knew I could not get loose. He said, "YOU HAVE TO DIE" since I would not obey, and no one would ever have me. He told me to grab my things, and he grabbed the back of my neck and made me pack my car. He dragged me up and down the stairs by the neck with my arms filled with my things to pack my car. He kept repeating over and over he was going to kill me. He would have me pick up my paycheck and then kill me and place my dead body in my car and put it in the woods.

After about nine trips up and down the apartment stairs, while his hand gripped my neck as I packed my car. I started thinking, "Am I going to die?" I needed to figure out how to live. Being dragged around like a rag doll and being punched was getting to be too much. Plus, packing the car and going up and down all the stairs was draining me. I started to see he was getting tired. So, he told me I could go downstairs on the next trip alone. When I made it to the fourth step, I ran to the apartment guard booth faster than Flo Jo ever ran. I pleaded with the guard to go to the leasing office and call the police. I could see shock in the man's face because of how beaten and bloody I appeared. I explained, "Don't help me just go call the police, or he will assault you too." I then locked myself in the guard booth. The guard ran to the office to call for help. My boyfriend ran to the guard booth and raised his hand to punch the glass. I shrank down to the floor. My mind was made up that I would die in that guard booth today. He would not take me back to the apartment no matter what he did.

As I sat terrified and bloody on the floor of the apartment guard shack, my mind was thinking I do not want to die. Is this man trying to kill me? I heard police cars speed past the guard shack into the apartment complex, but I was too afraid to get up off the floor and see what was happening. All my mind could concentrate on was "I am not dead." But clearly, I was broken. The police came to get me out of the guard booth. I was shaking uncontrollably and very afraid to stand up. The officer told me my abuser was in a police car and could not hurt me. He asked if I had someplace to go because I only had fourteen hours and they would release him. At that moment, I decided I wanted to live, and I would find somewhere to go. My car was packed, and there were only a few things left for me to grab. I drove to a friend's house to sleep and hide until I could get rest. I had been up over twenty-four hours by this time.

Once I was able to get the rest I needed, the next morning I drove back to Houston to stay with my mom. For a year, I hid. I did not work or stay alone anywhere. I went to work with friends and followed my mom everywhere she went because fear had me so bound. My mind kept telling me he was coming for me and going to kill me. It took me about three years to return to the Dallas/Fort Worth area without being afraid.

I know you are wondering what got me here. Well, from the moment I saw him, I knew he was a football player. He was physically fit and large in stature. His shy but sexy smile drew me in, and his smooth way of talking to me was the icing on the cake. In the beginning, he made me feel I was important to him, and he never wanted to live without me. I could tell he was hurting, but I did not know why. He treated me as though

I was a trophy that only he could touch and put on display. He would invite his friends over and have me put on short shorts and a crop top to show my body to his friends. At first, I thought it was strange, but I did it anyway. Just what he wanted to happen happened. The men would comment how sexy I was, and he would be smiling and happy. He had me serve them all drinks and stay in the living room silent while they all talked. Little did I know he was setting me up. After all the company left, he started pushing me around accusing me of looking at one of his friends. I was so confused, and I explained I would never do that. He called me a liar and said he saw me looking at the guy. Then POW! He punched me. I screamed and kneeled down on the floor, trying to understand what was happening. I was crying and hoping I would not get hit again. He instantly apologized and said he did not know why he did that. I was so lost that I did not know how to respond, so I believed him and forgave him.

As time progressed, the hitting did not end, and it was a new situation every time the abuse happened. I was so afraid of him that I walked around like I was walking on eggshells. One day, I decided to ask him why he was so angry. He began to explain and showed me a photo book of football clippings of him as a college football star heading to the NFL. Then I saw rage in his eyes when he said NFL, and that is when he slammed the photo book down and got mad at me. I tried to reason with him, and he kept screaming at me about why I brought any of this stuff up. I explained, while crying, I just wanted to understand him. That is when he started to sling me around like I was a rag doll and threw me down repeatedly on the floor. I yelled and blocked as many punches as I could, not understanding what happened and why he was going crazy on me. Just as fast as it started, it ended. And he began to sob, screaming "I will never be anything."

Now, I must be a crazy fool because as beat up as I was by him, I now tried to comfort and console him. As he sobbed, he began to say, "The last game I played in college right before I was supposed to sign the NFL contract, I damaged my knee. It was damaged so badly that I left in an ambulance off the field during the game. The doctor told me I would never play football again. So, my life is over." He then went on to tell me he was taking it all out on me even though he knows it is wrong but wanted it to stop. So, of course, like an idiot, I decided to stay with him not realizing this man needed serious counseling. I thought just loving him would help him see past his hurt, and we could make it work.

Well, I was mistaken. I got slapped because his barber asked about me while he was cutting his hair at the barbershop. He continued to hit me and accuse me of having an affair with the barber. I was screaming, crying, and blocking punches again, asking him how I could be cheating when he knew where I was every minute of the day. As I cried and screamed, he snapped and realized I was right; he timed my every move. So, here we go again with the apologizing which I was growing extremely sick of. Here I go again, believing it would never happen again.

However, this time I had a doctor's appointment the next day. Not realizing how beaten up and battered my body was, I still went to the appointment. As soon as the doctor began the examination, she asked me if I was okay. I, of course, said I was good. She stated not from the look of my face and body. Then she began to tell me that I did not deserve to be treated like that, and she knew where I could go to get help. I had grown tired of all the sporadic beatings and wanted something different, but I did not know how to leave. She told me to just drive straight there after our appointment, and they would help me from there. Without giving it a second thought, I drove to the shelter. As I entered the shelter, my mind was racing.

"What am I doing? How will I get my things? Am I seriously leaving him? Will he look for me?" As thoughts continued to bombard my mind, I settled into the shelter and decided to just stay. I no longer wanted to be hit. However, the next morning when it was time for breakfast, my mind began to question, "Do I belong here?" All the women there were married with children, and none of them worked. I was dressed in a suit and heading to work after breakfast. I had no children, and I had never been married. So, my mind was telling me I do not belong. Then the woman sitting next to me must have seen my facial expression and said, "You are not different than us." I turned and said, "Yes, I am." She said, "No, you are not. We all have experienced abuse, and I see the bruises on you." I then explained, "But you all depend on someone to take care of you and your children, and I work and provide for myself." At that moment, I wanted to go back because I thought a shelter was not for me.

Well, when I got off work and went back to the apartment, he was sitting there looking as though he was sad. He was remorseful and said he thought I had left him. I was immediately drawn back into caring about his feelings and tried desperately to console him. I think that lasted two days and once again I was abused. This time, the barber came to visit and asked him where I was. He called me out of the room, and the barber's face lit up from seeing me. I began to cry inside because I knew I would once again get beaten. As I predicted, the minute the barber left the apartment, he started punching me. He screamed, "I knew you were cheating, and that day you were gone you were with him. You lied about being at a shelter." I was crying and trying to explain I could take him to the shelter to show him where I was. He stated, "Did you see how he lit up when you came out of the room?" I said, "No, I did not see anything." The beating, kicking, punching, and throwing me around continued. He said, "He will never have you; I will kill you first."

Kill me was all I could think about the next few days. Now, I needed to produce a plan to leave. I was not sure if he would try to kill me, but the blows I kept taking sure felt like it. This was when the pivot came into my life, and I truly needed help. Although I did not die that day, I was dead inside. It took a marriage filled with abuse and another attempt on my life for me to get help. I realized I was the common denominator, and I did not want to die. So, I went to individual counseling and group counseling and read books, so my life would change. I decided I wanted to live and be healthy and not be beaten to death. I learned so much about myself getting counseling. I learned how to see the red flags that men display, so I would not be abused physically again.

My encouragement to other women is to never give up on yourself. You cannot change or help someone who does not want it. However, you can help better yourself. You can change and learn to live a healthier life. I have not been in a physically abusive relationship for over twenty-five years. I know if God did it for me, He will do it for you too. We are all created in His image, and I needed to start believing it. Counseling can help you see where change needs to be made in your life, and God will help you change if you want to. Do not ever feel you deserve abuse of any form whether physical, mental, emotional, sexual, or verbal. Learn to love yourself, so your children are not a victim of the cycle you lived through. Get a mentor who will walk alongside you to help you. There are several resources in place now to assist you and your children in getting to a better place.

Do not live in fear any longer. Believe in yourself and get the help you and your children need. Love does not involve abuse of any kind. Love is an action not just words. Look at yourself in the mirror and love who you are.

Lisa's Bio

Lisa Evans, a God-fearing single parent of five, turned her trials into triumph through her faith, fortitude, and friendships. Born in San Francisco, California but reared in Houston, Texas, Lisa has earned a BA in English, a BS in Christian leadership and a master's in business administration. She is an evangelist who encourages women to live through faith and not abuse.

Lisa is currently a real estate broker and a director of Evans Employment Enterprises. She is devoted to sharing her story of surviving domestic violence and living life to the fullest. She has her own 501c3, S.P.R.OUT Foundation, which supports women going through domestic violence. She has shared her story at the Star of Hope, the Debra Duncan Show, KTSU radio station, and on several podcast stations.

Lisa is a devoted advocate for ending domestic violence and lives by the fact that she is not different from anyone else. She just does not give up regardless of what obstacles come her way because God is truly her source.

Contact and Booking Information
Instagram: @iamlisawevans
Email: les.p.r.out@gmail.com

WALKING IN MY TRUTH AND OVERCOMING TRIGGERS

By Rianne Egana

I often reflect on how I got here. Why am I still alive? Knowing I did not do my part in protecting myself. I've dealt with trigger responses for years.

I will always remember those tragic events that changed my life and got me back into fellowship with God.

I started understanding these triggers two years ago as I laid in a chair at the dentist office. The doctor was viewing X-rays of multiple side-lined abscesses in my mouth. He asked me if I had been in a car accident. Mind you, I was two years out of my abusive relationship, so I couldn't do anything but cry. I knew where the trauma to my face came from. I couldn't believe that I had finally escaped it, and I was still dealing with the health issues. I responded no to the dentist. It brought me back to that day as the tears started to roll down my cheeks.

I no longer recognized my smile while brushing my teeth. See, years before, he smashed a tablet in my face. I drove myself to urgent care while holding my lip together as blood continued to trickle down my shirt. They applied several stitches. Another time, my tooth was broken off to the gum line, and the pulp on neighboring teeth was draining into my face, causing extensive swelling. With nerve damage to my lip, I stopped smiling often because I noticed it was no longer my God-given one. He tried to damage an internal smile that could never be broken. The punches to my face became the easiest way to quiet me during arguments. I had become numb walking into work with the excuse that I ran into the door.

I thought back to my son's birthday party months earlier, and I had sensed then that he was involved with someone again. He had threatened to throw bleach on me while I was in the tub. We cursed at each other, then he suddenly put up his fists to fight me but instead tried to spit on me, grabbing a can of bathroom cleaner and sprayed it. I gagged, inhaling chemicals and pushed him away. Even though we were just minutes away from leaving for our son's party, I cleaned myself up and departed in separate cars. I was withdrawn at the party because I was reliving painful moments and tried to pretend they never happened. I suddenly needed to leave; something was wrong. My breathing deteriorated while driving to urgent care. I hoped different nurses were on staff as I was now a repeat visitor. I told them I inhaled cleaning chemicals. After receiving a steroid shot and oxygen, I was put on an albuterol sulfate inhalant and diagnosed with chemically induced pneumonia. I spent over three months on inhalers. Years later, this triggers anxiety as COVID mandated wearing masks and was enforced heavily. It caused anxiety because I knew it was reducing my normal breathing patterns further.

The woman they thought had it all together was slowly dying inside an abusive relationship, hiding the bruises from the world. I think about the times I left but returned after he apologized telling me he never wanted to lose me. I was asked before how many times I went back. I was ashamed to say I went back repeatedly because I loved him. I prayed for him to change. The real answer was too many times.

See, I had given up hope; I had quit. I was no longer living, but I was surviving. But over these last few healing years not only did I have to recognize my faults, but I also had to completely rebuild myself, while grounding my children who were also dealing with the traumatic aftereffects. I abstained from dating to heal myself not wanting to carry anything over to a deserving man God sent into my life.

I had to acknowledge the fact I had been through severe narcissistic abuse. I had to stop hiding what happened to me to move past my shame. The aftermath was very difficult as I dealt with relationship abandonment and being separated from people I thought were friends. Through it all, I was suffering with PTSD and these triggers I dealt with in silence.

The abuse I suffered was primarily behind affairs he had been having when I got in the way. The women he was messing around with were now pranced around in public and accepted as if I didn't even exist. Too many lies were told, while I had to shelter our son from all the wickedness.

We don't talk about this enough, but I was trauma bonded. I made a decision to either go with what society expects you to do or turn it all over to God. I heard the whispers calling me a liar; I heard the false statements that I was trying to destroy someone's character. I was even told to be quiet about it all. They plotted against me and meddled for personal gain, which had me pondering if I would even have a fair chance in court. The public circle had shifted. Nobody came to rescue me, and even if they did, would I have been ready?

I heard and saw it all. Why? Because I chose God, I chose to do something I was never taught to do. And God revealed all to me. He provided all the answers needed. God showed His hand. He showed me everyone's place in my life. You see, He already prepared that table in front of my enemies (Psalm 23:5). He sustains me, and I know vengeance is His.

That walk hasn't been easy. I have suffered setbacks, sometimes giving into the flesh delaying my journey. But God has always reached back to lift me up again. He is a restorer.

I asked the questions, "How are you going to cheat on me? Abuse me? Lie to me and mistreat me for years?" Then you elevate a Jezebel to hurt me.

I didn't understand why these women would meet my now ex-spouse during the day. Even though they knew of me, it didn't matter to them. They were blinded with lust, not knowing the dark secrets of pain I was carrying. They wanted the façade. Then I finally had to let it all go.

Women were hurting women instead of holding him accountable. I was reminded to stop expecting your morals from others. They choose to engage in ungodly behavior. What they are blinded from realizing is they are acting against God's chosen, working together like Jezebel and Ahab throughout our divorce process.

They put their mouths on me without having all the facts and ignored the main fact that there was a covenant made in marriage that was replaced with abuse, adultery, and sin.

God watches everything when you take part in acts against a person using Jezebel. These women who were helping him with the intent to hurt me wanted a position. They tried to compete where they can't even compare. They are going to suffer the same consequences, if not worse, for helping him because everything was done to not only hurt me, but they also hurt children. They conspired to not have a praying child sleep in his own bed to make way for their own.

I can't tell you how many nights I had to comfort our son to sleep while his world was turned upside down, and he felt abandoned and afraid he'd lose me too. I supported him through counseling, while doing the most to hide my pain.

Women are nurturers and to take a position to hurt another woman and her kids, knowing what that feels like, is demonic. Spiritual warfare was so evident, trying to break me. But it was more so to hurt and break these kids. See, if you break the man, you break his home. It was never about me. This man held the door open for all the attacks. They hurt God before they hurt me.

I learned to not envy those women or that woman that decided to stay because she knows what he's done. Her self-esteem is in hell; she doesn't love herself, and she's so thirsty and desperate to cling onto him even though she saw what he did to me. She knows he beat me. She knows he cheated because she was helping him cheat, even while he cheated on her. I was removed from all the toxic triangulations.

Kingdom men and women should have maturity for themselves, marriage, and God. I understand nobody is perfect in a sin-sickened world, but we have got to do better. God's ordaining of marriage is a beautiful thing. Not every day is easy, and it takes work. Don't defile marriages for others because you don't want to respect yours or someone hurt you. I took a stance. There is no room for abuse or adultery. It could've been a battle of evils, but instead, I turned to God, refusing to accept the attacks of the enemy. What did it profit to try to destroy me out of jealousy and wickedness? To expose my health? Was the public embarrassment needed?

God has vindicated me because I got away. I didn't have to break anyone else down, and I didn't need to put my hands on anyone. I packed up my stuff and left with my self-respect.

Forgiveness was key along my journey of healing from shame. As women and mothers, we protect our families. We become the role models they look up to while in need of more male role models to set a positive example. I often hear children are resilient and will be okay, but it's the children that suffer greatly in silence from broken homes. Through our distractions, we deprive them of our best selves, not providing the nurturing they deserve. Without it, they feel rejected, carrying those burdens into their teen years when the aftermath comes out. They are child victims of domestic violence. This is what you see evidenced in our streets today due to the lack of love and empathy for lives. We have to set better examples, especially for these youth we are losing.

We have to pour into them recognizing the trauma these kids are facing daily. These children and teens who have dealt with trauma often develop PTSD by the time they graduate. It starts at home. This is why we have to shift that focus.

We have to teach ourselves to love ourselves again and to heal before starting a new relationship. No, nobody's perfect, and we have all made mistakes, but God's love for us is amazing. You see, I now understand I was broken too, which is why I endured a toxic relationship for so long, feeling desperate for a family. What if God had given up on me when I was in the world?

Twenty-eight years ago, I found myself homeless as a teenager. On my graduation day, I recall catching the bus to the auditorium dressed in a borrowed dress, hoping nobody would see me getting off the bus. My cap and gown hidden in a bag, I was embarrassed by having to find my way there, knowing nobody would be there to support me. Entering the auditorium, I saw graduates and families filling the room, while longing for family of my own to support me. I thought of my siblings who had entered the foster care system and were facing the same issues. Through it all, I was graduating, and that was something to be proud of. Tears rolled down my face while I walked across that stage. The lack of support back then made me push harder to hold it together.

God was always there, but I resisted Him. I was worried about the material things keeping me there. Every time I received a sign, I second-guessed it and was afraid to start over, ignoring God's will for me. Until July 3, 2019, I was on my knees in tears praying over an open Bible and was led to Scriptures. They still resonate with me to this day. There were humbling messages encouraging me to put my complete faith and trust in Him. I started my journey of healing. I finally got the courage to walk away, leaving it all behind, the house, the furniture, and my life as I knew it. We moved with just our clothes packed into a car he later demanded back.

God, in turn, placed me in rooms with great women, and His perfect alignment was right on time... women empowering women. My restoration has been amazing, and He is not done yet.

Something beautiful shifted in me. I found peace. I found purpose.

I returned the car he had initially bought for me, and God replaced it. I lost our house, and God gave me a home. I started a new life. Using my financial knowledge, I was able to better ground myself.

I was introduced to our visionary author, Dr. Yolanda J. Henderson, who started an anthology highlighting domestic violence. When I started writing my story, I found the power of my voice. I rediscovered myself. I remembered who I am and who God created me to be. See, my story was never meant for me; my story was meant to help others. God brought me to Psalm 105 in the middle of the day in that temporary apartment. It was one of the most vivid, beautiful visions I had ever had, realizing at that moment, all would be well.

"Give thanks to the Lord and call out to Him! Tell the nations what He has done! Sing to Him; sing praises to Him. Tell about the amazing things He has done. Be proud of His holy name. You followers of the Lord, be happy! Depend on the Lord for strength. Always go to Him for help. Remember the amazing things He has done. Remember His miracles and His fair decisions. You belong to the family of His servant Abraham. You are descendants of Jacob, the people God chose. The Lord is our God. He rules the whole world. He will remember His agreement forever. He will always keep the promises He made to His people" (Psalm 105:1-8, ERV).

Yes!!! He said, "Don't hurt my chosen people. Don't harm my prophets."

I went on to receive coaching certifications by the amazing Dr. Shekina Farr who encouraged me on my journey to impact other people's lives, working more deeply rooted in the community, helping where I could motivate and inspire. My walk hasn't been easy. I have suffered setbacks, at times, giving in, filled with doubt. But God has always reached back to lift me up again. He is a restorer.

I'm helping women see that it is okay to not be okay and exemplifying that grace, mercy, and favor does exist. Hope surrounds us all. Oftentimes, we are hidden in plain sight to protect and mold us into who we are becoming, reminding us that we no longer have to live in shame. Cycles are ready to be broken. We are generational curse breakers. Women have to guide, nurture, and love our children to be the best versions they can be.

I've touched lives by not giving up when I wanted to, even when I didn't know people were watching. I remember the pastor's wife giving me a card on Women's Day. I was in tears throughout the entire sermon, reflecting on and ashamed of how many times I thought God had given up on me. I didn't open it until after the service. As I continued to weep, I read the note. "Thank you for your example of GRACE UNDER FIRE "

The card included the Scriptures, Philippians 3:17 and 1 Peter 2:19-21. "One of you might have to suffer even when you have done nothing wrong. If you think of God and bear the pain, this pleases God. But if you are punished for doing wrong, there is no reason to praise you for bearing that punishment. But if you suffer for doing good and you are patient, this pleases God. This is what you were chosen to do. Christ gave you an example to follow. He suffered for you. So you should do the same as he did:" (1 Peter 2:19-21, ERV).

Leading by example, it was right on time. Love yourself and know what they tried didn't work. When you see me, I want you to see what God has done for me. When you have to steal, manipulate, and play games to get ahead, you are already losing. No matter how many lies are told and how timelines are changed to justify wrongs, you look foolish explaining and twisting them, especially when the truth is and will always be the truth. God always reveals. I didn't listen before, wanting to do things my way. But I know when I surrendered, He welcomed me back as I am.

I now stay close to my family and the people in my life that stuck around. We have to remember to always stay close to our morals and our integrity. Hold close to your light, your joy, your faith, and your hope. Those morally corrupt that tried to hurt me have been placed on the altar. God holds us accountable.

Isaiah 54:4-5 reminds us not to be afraid! It told me that I would not be disappointed, and people would not say bad things against me. It was a reminder that I would not be embarrassed. When I was young, I felt shame, but it was now time for me to forget that shame. God's Word told me that I would not remember the shame that was felt when I lost my husband. My real husband is the one who made me. His name is Lord all-powerful. The Holy One of Israel is your protector, He is the God of all the earth!

"Like a woman whose husband left her you were very sad. You were a young wife left all alone. But the Lord has called you back to him" (Isaiah 54:6).

This is what God also says in Isaiah 54:7-8. "For a short time, I turned away from you, but with all my love I will welcome you again. I was so angry that for a while I did not want to see you. But now I want to comfort you with kindness forever." The Lord your Savior said this.

I will continue to glorify God, walking in His light. I now have appreciation instead of expectations. Self-care and loving yourself is crucial to healing. When you see me now, I am looking and feeling better than ever because I am cultivating joy. God saved my life!

I'm here to tell you to let your healing journey begin.

Rianne's Bio

Rianne Egana is an accomplished vice president in commercial lending with a heavy focus on building banking relationships, networking, and community outreach. She has more than twenty-five years of extensive experience in financial consulting, which has helped countless small business owners and individuals with business growth, lending, and being successful in expanding their opportunities.

Through her drive and willingness to always help others excel and impact the community, she also founded her business B2B Waymaker, which is geared towards serving underprivileged minority youth and helping young adults gain access to tutoring, life skills sessions, and motivational seminars to assist with personal development and career readiness.

She is also working with Thrive New Orleans helping BIPOC and re-entry citizens with job placement, financial literacy, and credit solutions.

Rianne is currently attending Tulane University furthering her education and is a graduate of Formidable Coaching Institute where she holds several certifications as a certified business development coach, certified life skills coach, and certified youth empowerment coach.

She was featured in Formidable Woman Magazine as part of "Power 20": Accomplished Women in Different Industries. She is also a best-selling co-author of *My Walk Past Hell* anthology, which highlights domestic abuse and becoming an overcomer.

Likewise, she is an international best-selling co-author of *A Joyful Heart,* exploring reflections of overcoming life's challenges through God's amazing grace.

She has three wonderful kids, two who have already graduated with great accomplishments of their own. She is an active member of Franklin Avenue Baptist Church in New Orleans.

Contact and Booking Information
Email: Rianne@b2bwaymaker.com
Website: www.b2bwaymaker.com

RESPECT THE RED FLAGS

By Selika Corley-Funchess

Will this night ever end? My body cannot endure any more of this. I have begged for my life for the past four hours, yet it continued. I had the opportunity to look in the mirror, and I was horrified at my reflection. My head was swollen. My face was bloody. My hands were swollen. My entire body was sore. Breathing was painful. All I could do was cry.

I've heard you never forget your first. It's true. I will never forget my first day of school, the first time I drove to school, and my first job. Of all the things I remember, I will never forget the first time I was abused.

If the tone in your voice rises, I'm nervous. If there is yelling or screaming, I'm immediately in survival mode. Why am I this way? As the result of years of abuse, I have multiple mental health diagnoses.

I was nineteen years old, and I thought I had my life together. There was nothing you could tell me because I was grown. I had just given birth to my first child, was working, and had found the one I was going to spend the rest of my life with.

The red flags were flying almost immediately. I was so blinded by what I thought was love that I didn't pay attention. It's a decision I regret to this day. He literally swept me off my feet. He was always present. I could guarantee that he would stop by my parent's house to see me when he got off from work. The compliments were flowing from his lips constantly. They made me feel good internally. We stayed on the phone for hours, or I was at his mother's house whenever I wasn't working. His timing was perfect. I was fresh out of a relationship that ended with a child. My child's father was my first love, and I didn't think I would ever get over that relationship.

How many red flags did you count? What I grew to understand is that his timing was perfect for predatory/abusive behavior. He knew my child's father and knew exactly when to start his action plan. He came to see me on his way home to ensure I was at home most of the time. He didn't have to worry about my location because I loved him. I would be at his mother's house until nine or ten at night. After I arrived home, we would spend half the night on the phone. That was a part of his controlling behavior. Knowing my every move fed his ego.

Our definition of love was different. I fell head over heels while he became more and more controlling. I couldn't tell the difference. I looked at them the same. Those compliments soon began to decrease in frequency. I went from the most beautiful girl in the world to being called some of the foulest names and being confronted with some of the most outlandish accusations I had ever experienced at the time. If I was at work for eight hours out of the day and with him for ten hours a day, there was no way I wasn't cheating the remaining hours of the day to him. In his warped mind, there was no way I was a faithful girlfriend. Women aren't faithful, at least not to him. I was running myself ragged to prove a point to someone who refused to change his mind about me. His perception was not my reality.

To please him, I distanced myself from friends and family. At that young age, I was a social butterfly. I loved my friends, traveling, and spending time with my family. Family was always big to me. They noticed when I stopped calling or attending regular events. My friends noticed as well. I didn't care about anything except making sure he was happy at the expense of my own happiness.

A short time into the relationship, I noticed his anger and outbursts. They were not directed towards me, but that did not last long. My turn came soon enough. The first time we had a serious argument, he got so angry that he punched me in my throat. I didn't know what to do. I stood there stiff as a board. Once the shock wore off, I remember asking why. He told me to just leave. Alone and afraid, I did as he asked. I questioned myself all the way. I blamed myself.

Soon after I arrived home, the phone started to ring. I was bombarded with "I love you" and "It will never happen again" and "I'm sorry." My emotions took over. Within a few days, I was right back with him. I found myself trying to keep him from becoming upset. It never worked. Nothing I did was good enough. The beatings progressively became more intense. I kept going back. My secret was safe because I was too ashamed to let anyone know what I was enduring. If I could just keep him happy, everything would be fine. I repeated this lie to myself for years. I suffered in silence.

Time went by, and the cycle kept repeating itself. While talking to his mother, it was revealed that his father was abusive to her as well. His father passed away when he was a toddler, so he never really knew him. Maybe what I was enduring was hereditary or generational, I guess. That conversation started me thinking. I started noticing the change in me then the reality of his abuse showed up. I couldn't look at myself in the mirror, and when I did, I didn't like what I saw. I didn't recognize myself. The more I was around him, the more I realized I spent years searching for the man I was originally introduced to. He was gone. I would never see the representation again, no matter how I waited for him to return.

One night, we attended a family function. He embarrassed me terribly that night, and I had reached my breaking point. I decided that I was going to end the relationship and move on with my life. I took a deep breath and told him I wanted out of the relationship. In his intoxicated state, he began beating me until I turned black, purple, and blue. I stared into his eyes, and they were empty. For the next four or five hours, I was beaten severely and not allowed to leave. I was beaten while driving, on a church property, and from one county to the next. When he was done, he asked me to continue keeping the same secret I hid all these years. Because I wanted to leave, I said I would.

The next morning, my parents were upset and all the people I had been alienated from showed up for me. I went to the emergency room because I was still hurting and swollen. The social worker came in while I was being examined by the doctor. She asked the question that almost every person who experienced trauma does not like to be asked, "Why didn't you leave?" My self-esteem had taken the same beating my body had taken. I was not given any referrals or offered services to help me begin to heal.

I filed a police report, and he was arrested. I did not know at the time the charges he had pending. His family later reached out to me to inform me of the charges. They came to me to ask me to drop the charges. I still loved him and hated what he did to me at the same time. I went before the judge and dropped the charges within the week. In about two weeks, we were back together. It only lasted a few months. I tried to end it again. This time he started hurting himself instead of me. That kept me running back until I finally said no more. I was tired, and I needed to heal. By the time I decided to end it, we had one child together. I found out afterwards that I was pregnant with another child that we share.

I moved out and attempted to move on with my life. He would sit at a store across the street from my apartment and would call me to let me know when I made it home or who was coming to visit me. I invited a friend over one night to watch a movie, and he was spotted outside my apartment, banging on the window and screaming. I was humiliated.

I was a single mother of three, healing and still vulnerable. I knew what an unhealthy relationship was, but I walked around branded like the woman with the scarlet letter. I attracted more of the same men for many years.

After years of failed, abusive relationships, I thought I finally found a winner. That's the furthest thing from the truth. I was love bombed so well until I had the wind knocked out of me. I ran into a high school friend, and it developed into a true relationship over time. He showered me with gifts, foot massages, and surprised me at work with lunch. There was nothing I couldn't ask for that he wouldn't get for me. We dated for several months until we were in a committed relationship.

He slowly started moving into my home that I shared with my children. It was good in the beginning. Suddenly, he began to tell me that women should respect their men. The male chauvinistic behaviors began. No sir! Ephesians 5:22 says, "Wives obey your husband..." There was no mention about a boyfriend. This is why you should read and understand the Bible for yourself. He twisted Scriptures to suit his purpose. Over time, he became emotionally and financially abusive. This was the first time I endured a situation like this. Often it's not recognized as abuse if it's not physical.

He found another home to move us into that was better than the previous one. I later found out from the landlord that he had not been paying rent as he promised. We were about to be evicted. The landlord offered to enter into a lease with me, but he could not remain in the home. I agreed and signed the new lease. I sat down to talk to him about the arrangement I made and served him with a notice to vacate as required by law. He became irate and began to throw things and break things in the house. I called for law enforcement, and they came to remove him from the property. I explained my side of what was going on, and they said they would take him in on the outstanding warrant he had. The officer told me to pack his things while he was in jail and be done with him. As soon as they pulled off, I began packing his car with as many of his belongings as I could. I pulled his car to the end of the driveway and left his keys with a relative. He continued to harass me months after until I filed an order of protection to keep him from popping up at the house and knocking on the door. My order was good for one year, and he eventually stopped.

Throughout those relationships, I ignored red flags. Each time, I felt as though I was blindsided because I loved someone who didn't love me. They loved my vulnerabilities. I loved them more than I loved myself. My self-esteem and self-worth were wrapped up in partners who didn't value me.

I share my testimonies for many reasons. My first reason is always to help someone. Dealing with abusers is life-changing, and it can be overwhelming. I survived, and you can too. If you are enduring a narcissist or abusive partner, seek help when you're ready to plan your exit.

You will need a strong support system to help you with safety planning and resources. Remember, there is power in the pen (ink pen). To prove verbal abuse, you must either have a witness or be able to prove the pattern of verbal abuse. Write down what was said, when it was said, and annotate if there are any witnesses.

If you need an advocate, check with your local shelter or law enforcement agency. They can help you navigate the court system and provide assistance in other areas. Make sure that with all of the services and resources you can receive therapy is included. Therapy and prayer are the reasons why I can help others and tell my story. I couldn't effectively break the cycle until I remembered whose I am.

My faith was the source of my strength and still is. Healing is not easy, but it is freedom. I am no longer bound by the chains of trauma and abuse. My walk past hell was difficult, but like Shadrach, Meshach, and Abednego, I don't even smell like smoke.

Selika's Bio

Selika Corley-Funchess has always been an advocate. Please don't mistake her smiles and calm demeanor as a sign of weakness. Selika is stronger than she appears. She has used her platform to educate the community on the rising crime of human trafficking. Selika has used her voice for those who have been silenced by their abusers, whether it was domestic violence or sexual assault.

She has used her voice in the courtroom, assisting victims of domestic violence with fighting for orders of protection, filing affidavits, or initiating peace bonds to protect men and women against further abuse.

Furthermore, she has worked tirelessly to train with other advocates, law enforcement agencies, colleges and universities, and other agencies to provide the best service possible to her clients. Selika often says, "I use my past experiences to help survivors feel understood and heard. I remember feeling alone when I was enduring trauma. I don't want anyone else to feel that way, ever."

Selika previously served as the victims assistance coordinator and certified crime prevention specialist for the local sheriff's office, crisis counselor with the local Rape Crisis Center, non-profit board member with YFOCUS, Inc., public speaker, and author.

It is not surprising that she has been featured in SwagHer Magazine, Mississippi Today, Mississippi Public Broadcast, 90.1 FM's Coffee & Conversation with Wanda Evers, and Woman to Woman with Joanne and Fox 8 (New Orleans), and various other forms of media.

She currently enjoys working with the seasoned population in the Social Services department of a local skilled nursing facility.

Contact and Booking Information
FaceBook: Selika Corley-Funchess
Instagram: Mypassionismypurpose

A NEW SITUATION... THE SAME MAN!

By Shellita Garrett

Walking up the stairs to a hairstylist's apartment, I heard the thumping bass coming from a 1982 Cutlass Supreme. A voice called out, "Hey Red," and I turned to see a man with a gleaming row of gold teeth smiling wide. We exchanged numbers, and within hours, I received a page on my beeper. That's when it all began – I became a drug dealer's girlfriend, immersed in a world of hidden money, extravagant shopping sprees, and the constant threat of danger.

I was a middle-class girl from New Orleans, raised on what they called the "White side" of every neighborhood we lived in. The drug game was entirely foreign to me. Late nights and days turned into nights, and the constant fear of law enforcement became my new reality. Riding around listening to Tupac, Mystikal, Hot Boyz, Bone Thugs & Harmony, and New Orleans bounce music, we made drug drops, always vigilantly looking for police. I was oblivious to the perilous environment I was in and the potential consequences of being caught with drugs.

As time passed, I began hearing rumors about other girls he was involved with. Initially, I brushed them off, but when I confronted him, he reacted with anger and aggression. He started controlling my movements, dictating who I could talk to, and forbidding me from going out when he wasn't around. He isolated me from friends, discouraged visits to my family, and imposed curfews. He instilled fear in me, threatening and occasionally physically abusing me.

One time he hit me all over my head, face, and body. I was in bed so bruised and sore, and he would come and apologize and say, "Sorry, I didn't mean to hit you, but I was just mad, and you were talking back." I thought to myself, "You are not my daddy," but I kept my mouth shut to avoid any additional drama. He got mad all the time; it was like he was looking for something to argue about, to find a reason to hit me to later justify it. I said I am going to bed, and he said, "Why did you go to see your little boyfriend today?" I said, "What? I've been home all day," and he got in my face and said, "If I ever catch you with a nigga, I am going to kill you bitch!"

He grabbed my hair and face with his hands. I had tears in my eyes because I didn't understand what I did to deserve this treatment and what I had gotten myself into. I thought to myself maybe he was just saying he would kill me if I left him, so I decided if he does this shit again, I am going to leave him.

I got a call informing me that he was in jail so, of course, I went to bail him out. He went to jail several times, and the last time, another woman showed up in court for him. I didn't know, but his mother knew of her. She was there because she was the other woman he messed with off and on. She sold dope too and had about five kids, and the last one was his. A baby I didn't know about… LOL! Yes, he got her pregnant while we were together and living together.

When he got out of jail, I asked him about the entire situation. Like any guilty person, he got very angry, and we got into a heated argument. I left to go to my mom's house. He followed me there, and I parked in the driveway. About five minutes later, he pulled up to the door not the driveway. He said to me, "Let me talk to you." We talked, and that was when he said if I didn't leave with him, he was going to kill my mom and my sisters. Yes, I left with him and followed him back home.

Things escalated further one day when he returned home high, acting bizarre and aggressive. I tried to walk away, but he pursued me into the kitchen. As I reached for ice in the freezer, he forcefully grabbed my face and pushed my head against the wall to get my attention. I stared into his eyes and ignored him, prompting him to strike me in the head. An inner shift occurred, and I retaliated, surprising him. My uncharacteristic blow left my left ear bleeding and my hearing impaired.

I had enough. It had been a cycle of abuse off and on with this man. I was tired, so I walked to the bedroom and began to pack my clothes. I was on the side of the waterbed, and I heard a click and saw a barrow in my face. I heard him say, "If you are thinking about leaving me, I will blow your fuckin' brains all over that closet door!" I saw his finger on the trigger, and he had a look in his eyes I had never seen before. He was biting his bottom lip, and I saw his top gold teeth, and his face had sweat balls rolling down it. I froze. I never had a gun pulled on me, and tears rolled down my face out of fear. I told him I didn't want to leave, but I was just saying that because I was mad at him. I told him, "You know I love you and would never leave you." I asked him to put the gun down. He said, "If you love me, why you are leaving me? You don't love me."

We went back and forth until I convinced him that I loved him and convinced him to lower the gun. That night I couldn't sleep, thinking about what just took place. He pulled a gun on me a few more times, and I said to myself, "I must get out of this relationship before he kills me." I had to plan my escape. I parked my car on the side of the apartment and waited until he left the house one day, and I climbed out of the bedroom window.

My next partner is my baby's father. We initially connected as friends through my older sister, who was dating his best friend. We hung out a lot, laughing and smoking weed like pals. I didn't envision him becoming my child's father.

One day, while high and taking antibiotics for bronchitis (unaware that it rendered my birth control ineffective), we slept together in a moment of carelessness.

I have an amazing son who's a true blessing to me. However, fast forward to the time when things took an unexpected turn. The man I once knew as kind and fun-loving turned into someone lazy, mean, insecure, and bipolar.

While I worked hard to support our son, he became increasingly controlling and aggressive. He'd pick fights over my appearance, belittling me. I even started changing how I dressed and didn't take care of myself like I used to and started to gain weight because I felt worthless. He physically abused me, and despite my mother's warnings, I believed him over her.

He controlled my finances and every aspect of my life, making me feel trapped and humiliated. One day, my mother noticed my bruised eye, and it was humiliating. Makeup couldn't conceal the extent of the damage.

The abuse began to harm my baby too. He hit me in front of our child, scaring him so much that our baby cried and reached out to me. That moment was a breaking point for me. I couldn't bear to let my child witness such abuse or see him in tears. It hurt me deeply to see him cry. So, I made the tough decision to end our relationship. Besides, he was already cheating on me and had another child just two years after our son was born.

After we broke up, one day my truck had a flat, and I had a new guy friend. He offered to pick me up from work, to go get my son from his paternal grandmother's house, and to take me to go and get my flat fixed afterwards. I thought nothing of it. I picked my son up. Of course, I wasn't going to downgrade.

My new friend had a very nice ride and baby daddy's rides were broke down. LOL! We pulled up, and I got out to go get my baby, and his daddy came to the door. Remind you all that he had a woman that he had been cheating on me with. He was still with her at the time. He says, "Who the fuck that nigga you got my baby around?" I just ignored him as I walked out and jumped into the truck, and my new guy friend said, "What's up?" to him out of respect as we drove off.

My cell phone was blowing up from baby daddy texting me back-to-back. He was going off, and I ignored him. I dropped my baby off with my mom, and we went to get my tire fixed. When I got home, my mom said my baby's daddy came by. I called him, and he asked me to come over to discuss what had just happened. I went to his house. I pulled up. I didn't see him at first then I saw a shadow, and he walked up and asked me to get out of the car. I got out, and he hit me and grabbed my neck and started choking me. He said, "I am going to kill you bitch!" and I fell to the ground. I told him I could not breathe, but he kept holding my neck. I felt faint, but I tried to get him off of me. I kicked, and he hit me again. My throat was hurting, I felt tired, and he started to run behind me with a bat, swinging it at me. He hit my car with the bat.

I drove to the police station to make a report, and he was driving behind me very fast. I made the report, and we had to go to the domestic violence consulting and before the judge. I told the judge I was completely done with him and feared him and got a protective order in place.

After more than fifteen years without an abusive relationship, I unexpectedly met a guy we'll call "Ladies Love." He wasn't my usual type, but we struck up a conversation, exchanged numbers, and he persisted in calling. One day while I was busy with art and cooking chili at home, he asked me out. Instead, I invited him over, and we had a great time.

We began spending more time together, enjoying each other's company, and eventually, he asked me to be his girlfriend. We shared many experiences, traveled, partied, shopped, cooked, and even dressed alike. I practically lived at his place.

I didn't have any idea who he was… OMG! Being with this man was so much fun until I got to know the other side of him. He was a great person, but there was one side of him you didn't want to meet. I met that person one day. This man had to be in control all the time. It was his way or no way. I did not see his game; he learns you and what you like and studies women well. He knew what to say, what to do to get you where he wants you, and he tells you everything you want to hear, making you think you are the only woman.

He had multiple women at one time thinking they were the only woman. That personality I was talking about, Baabe, (in my New Orleans accent). He needs an entire book himself. I thought things were going well. His phone vibrated all the time, but I never thought anything of it; I trusted him. I was always with him. He still found time to cheat. I still had my own place, and from time to time, I would stay at my house to give us a break and time to miss each other. He didn't like it when I went home, or at least that was the mind game he played sometimes.

He had women come over the days and times when I was at home. These women knew of me, but I didn't know they existed. It was a Saturday morning, I got up and wanted to surprise him with breakfast. I knocked, and his son answered the door and let me in. I walked up the stairs and knocked at his bedroom door, and he came to the door with his robe on.

He looked as if he saw his own ghost. I pushed to walk in, and he tried to hold me back. I did not notice the woman in his bed, yet his reaction made me look up, and there she was under the covers. I just dropped everything and said, "What the fuck is this?" And he said, "Why the fuck didn't you call?" I never called him, so I didn't know what he was talking about. I said, "She knows you have a girlfriend?" He said, "Yes." I was like WOW! I told him to tell her ass to leave. He got angry and told me I needed to leave. I refused. I said, "While she leaves, I will be downstairs." Of course, she left. We talked about that then the women issues kept coming in different situations.

One day I had enough, and I told him I was going home, and I was breaking up with him. He threw all my things out of his house and pushed me out of the door and hit me in my face, spit in my face, and called me a bitch. There was another time he got so mad at me after an argument he threw my head down, punched me, hit me all over my body, had me in a corner, and kicked me in my head and all over my body, and if I moved, he would get even angrier and hit me again. I was in a corner crying and abused, and I tried to go home. That entire week, I stayed at his house. I am sure he knew he didn't want my son or my friends to see my bruises. This man would get angry at me and hit me like I was his personal punching bag.

Whatever he was upset about he took it out on me and blamed me for everything. One day, he hit me because he said I talked back and didn't listen to him. And I said I was going home, and he pushed me out of his house and ripped my clothes off, so I would be outside half-naked. My stuff was thrown all over in front of his house, and he pushed me, not allowing me to walk out like a normal person would do. I got a scar on my right foot on my big toe from when I had to get stitches because he beat me up and pulled me out of his house and dragged me, and my foot got cut on his screen door. He hit me on the head with a laptop multiple times while I was sitting down on the sofa because we were in an argument, and he didn't like what I said to him.

This got old, and I thought to myself, "What the fuck am I doing? I don't need him." I left him. It was not easy. It was five and a half years of my life off and on.

I decided to try something new. I decided to look on a dating site. I met the fourth guy. What a joke! He was an alcoholic. He hit me and cut me with a pocketknife on my hand. That was enough!! This relationship was very short-lived.

I believe that everyone is entitled to their own opinions, and I see all my choices as valuable life lessons. Some people are adept at making wise choices, while others, like me, sometimes go with the flow and give people chances even when there are red flags. Occasionally, we either don't notice those warning signs or are too vulnerable to acknowledge them initially.

I had a significant gap in years before entering another abusive cycle. What I've come to realize is that I've accepted men into my life who aren't on the same spiritual level and don't truly understand me as a woman. I possess strength and qualities that can be intimidating to many. I'm direct, independent, successful, charming, intelligent, and ever-changing. Most men can't handle the multifaceted person that I am, and this can lead to a desire for control.

I'm a Leo, and if there's one thing anyone knows about a lioness, it's that she can't be tamed by force. I need love, understanding, and connection. Attempts to control me only ignite my resistance, and I may engage in provocations just to challenge your dominance. I've reached a point in my life where self-love is my sanctuary. I've realized that I've been self-sufficient all my life, and these men bring nothing but turmoil. I don't want to share my time or energy with anyone who can't match my value.

I come from a royal bloodline and believe in manifesting my desires. God has reminded me repeatedly that I shouldn't waste my energy on these men who contaminate my spirit. I have a purpose, and the right man will respect and cherish me, enhancing my life rather than hindering it. He will prioritize my well-being, understanding my value and appreciating my journey.

In this phase of my life, self-love and self-care are my priorities. I'm committed to fulfilling my purpose, and I won't settle for anything less than a partner who supports and complements my path.

Shellita's Bio

Shellita Garrett, a native of New Orleans, Louisiana, discovered her unique ability to connect with the spiritual realm at a remarkably young age, around three or four years old. Throughout her childhood, she keenly sensed that she was set apart from the ordinary.

As she grew older, her spiritual gifts only grew more pronounced, compelling her to embark on a profound spiritual journey.

In the wake of the devastating Hurricane Katrina, Shellita found herself deep in prayer within the confines of a church in Longview, Texas, in a solitary moment that would alter the course of her life. It was during this solitary contemplation that she received a divine message from God urging her to journey westward.

This pivotal moment marked the genesis of her remarkable odyssey, commencing at the age of thirty in the vibrant Dallas/Fort Worth area.

Texas, with its abundant opportunities, proved to be an instrumental chapter in Shellita's life. She embraced the role of a devoted single mother, nurturing her son in this dynamic state.

Moreover, she seized the chance to further her education, ultimately obtaining a degree in criminal justice and a diverse array of certifications.

Her commitment to her academic pursuits also culminated in the attainment of an associate of applied science (AAS) degree in paralegal studies.

Contact and Booking Information
Email: shellitagarrett@yahoo.com
Instagram: @creolelady777

MALICIOUS INTENT

By Tinya L. Landry

I jumped up, heart pounding, pulse racing. I had to be dreaming. But then I heard it again. Banging, early in the morning. Desperate sounding, loud, official sounding. I was trembling, wondering who was at the door and why they were banging with such a sense of urgency. I slid out of bed, peeking in on my baby, and I tiptoed to the door to look through the peephole. Outside, I saw my friend, Elena, pacing back and forth frantically. As she reached to bang on the door again, I unlocked the door and opened it. She pretty much fell in the door, "Ho, you okay?" She was squeezing me so tightly; she was shaking and sweating, and I was trying to figure out what she was talking about. Her English was limited, so she took out a newspaper and put it in my face.

There in black and white was his photo, name, last known address, and the words, FORCIBLE RAPE OF A JUVENILE, in the most wanted section of the city's newspaper. My heart sank, I suddenly felt hot, and my legs felt weak. I managed to get to the sofa and sit down, holding the newspaper, wondering what in the world was going on.

How did I get here?

I got pregnant out of wedlock, and as a result, I was told that I needed to get in front of the church, confess, and ask for forgiveness or leave. Forgiveness? Mmmmm, okay. I was not going to do that, so I was put out. What was even worse, my mother was being disassociated with because I was still living at home. I felt so bad, heartbroken, because people that I loved and thought loved me abandoned me. It wasn't that they took care of me, but I loved them and thought they loved me. Their fellowship was important to me, my extended family. I called him, my daughter's dad, and told him what was up. He was like, "I got you and my baby, BLANK them. We don't need them." Soon after, we moved in together, and life was good...for a while.

My child's father started to change the more my pregnancy progressed. He was angry, unkind, and acting selfishly. It wasn't anything that I was able to put my finger on, but he was changing. I was doing laundry one day and found a receipt. I called the number, and it was one of those seedy Chinese massage parlors. He started going to strip clubs, just acting like someone I didn't know. My pregnancy was rough, I had that horrible never-ending morning sickness, but I wanted to get

106

out of the house sometimes too. One day, we went for a ride, and ended up at this hang out spot near a lake. He saw a few friends, so he walked off with them and left me sitting there by myself for quite some time.

A few guys saw me just sitting, realized that I was pregnant, and offered me a bottle of water. I took the water and thanked them. As I was drinking, he came back, smacked the bottle out of my hand, and said, "Let's go!" As we drove away, he accused me of trying to mess with those guys. He kept asking me their names and if the baby I was carrying was for one of them. I was shocked and told him he was acting crazy. He started shoving me in my head, pressing my face against the window hard, telling me I haven't seen crazy yet. He then drove to a part of town that wasn't so safe and tried to put me out of the car. I was terrified. I begged him to stop and to take me home. He had been drinking, so when we finally got home, I took a bath and tried to act like nothing happened. The next day, he was fine.

He continued to come and go as he pleased until one day I told him that I was sick of being left alone. He and I started arguing, and I threw a video tape at him as he started walking out the door. He charged at me, and I tried closing myself in the closet, but he busted in and choked me until I was blacking out. I tried to pry his arm from around my neck because he had me in a headlock. I managed to say, "What about the baby?" in a desperate attempt to breathe, and he let me go. I coughed and coughed and gasped for air. He left, and I cried as I called my parents. My daddy went to his job the next day with his gun and had a few words with him. I was told that I could always come home, but with the guilt and shame of being pregnant and unmarried, I felt like I was supposed to stay, so I stayed.

As time passed, we went to parenting classes, baby safety classes, practiced using the stroller, attended Lamaze classes, and did everything else having to do with our impending delivery. We seemed to be happy. One evening we went to a parade. He loved marching bands so as the bands came, he started to follow them. I couldn't keep up, so I was left alone again. As I was standing there, a man bumped into me and as he was saying, "Excuse me, I'm sorry sweetheart," I looked up at the man as I was about to tell him it was okay. I noticed who the man was. It was my biological dad. He didn't even recognize me until I called him by his name. We stood there catching up for a minute. I was so hurt that he didn't even know who I was, his own flesh and blood. As we were wrapping up our conversation, he came back. I introduced him to my biological dad, they shook hands, and he was off. We got in the car, and I broke. We never discussed me bumping into my dad, but I had to tell that part, so you would be able to put the pieces together later.

Fast forward, I had a beautiful baby girl. We were proud parents, and it was our first time getting out of the house. One day, we went by his parents' house, and the doorbell rang. He stepped outside to talk to whoever was at the door. On another day a month or so after, we wanted to be tourists in our city. We dropped the baby off at his parents' and had a wonderful afternoon of lunch, sightseeing, live music, etc. We got back to his parents' house, and it was total chaos! His mom was yelling and cussing, hitting him, telling us to leave and not come back. At this point, I was so confused and scared. What was I missing?

Elena knocking on the door and the newspaper filled in all of the blanks. That evening when he got home from work, I showed him the paper and told him not to lie to me. He confessed that he tried to have sex with a girl that was "red with a big ass." A stranger. I did the math. The event took place when our daughter was just ten days old! I was sick to my stomach. He had a look in his eyes; he was afraid. I never saw him so scared, but he was facing ninety-nine years in prison if tried and convicted. He fell to his knees, held my legs, and cried for what seemed like hours.

He begged me not to leave him, so I stuck by him. I wanted God to forgive me, so I tried to forgive him. I made it a point to be at every meeting with his lawyer because I didn't trust anyone, and I did not want to be kept in the dark. I heard every detail of how he tried having sex with this girl, twice in his car on his lunch break. I could barely function because I was so hurt and humiliated. We were both pretty popular and so everywhere I went, I got pity looks from people, and it was all I could stand to maintain my sanity. Everyone that I saw that fit that description, I wondered if it was her. I never got to see her. I had a funny feeling in the pit of my stomach that just never went away. He promised that we would move away and start a new life as a happy family as soon as things were straight.

I was so humiliated and hoping to escape this nightmare, so like a fool, I married him. I didn't know about making excuses for him, but the words from a few of the church members stayed on my mind. The main ones were that all my sins would fall on my baby because I got pregnant outside the will of God. I was willing to do whatever it took to be a good mother to my baby.

After we relocated, things were good. The charges were dismissed, and he seemed to be the model husband until he wasn't. We got pregnant again about a year or so after our move. We went for a prenatal visit, and to my heartbreak, our baby didn't have a heartbeat. I was devastated, but he smiled and said he dodged a bullet. I couldn't believe what I heard. I had to walk around with a dead baby inside of me. I went into labor before the break of day Christmas morning, and after I got in a room, he left me at the hospital, and I gave birth to a stillborn alone. After that, his behavior became more and more menacing. He liked to play mind games with me.

He started coming home late if at all, not wearing his ring (I can't believe that was even a thought), being disrespectful. As he started walking like a duck and quacking like a duck, I withdrew my affections. It hurt, but I was not going to be the

109

faithful wife at home while he was out in the streets doing God knows what with who knows who. He paid all of the bills, so he felt like that gave him license to be as disrespectful as he wanted.

One time we got into an argument, yelling and screaming, and some spit flew from my mouth, so he took the opportunity to spit in my face. He knew I had been sexually assaulted and by whom, and he told me that was the only person that wanted me. He started giving out our home phone number to different women. They would call and ask for a random name, and when I would ask them to describe the person that they were calling for, they described him perfectly. He didn't care how he treated me or about the things that he said to me. He slept with one of my coworkers and tried denying it with a smirk on his face, not knowing I had proof. He played mind games. My biological dad died, and I was making plans to go to the funeral, and he said, "I don't know what you crying for. That n$@@# didn't give a BLANK about you. I did more for you than he did. You need to be calling me daddy!" The words were vile and hurtful.

When people think about domestic violence, they think physical aggression, but he tormented me. I was full of guilt, shame, and rage, which then turned to self-doubt and insecurity. He made me feel worthless and unlovable. He told me that he went after the "red girl with the big ass" because I was nothing, and I wasn't even worth the wait. Our daughter was ten days old, and he said that waiting six weeks to have sex with me was a waste of time. After he got off with those charges, he became so arrogant and malicious. I couldn't believe that I ever got involved with someone like him. I never really knew him, and he certainly never cared anything about me.

I kept asking him to just leave. I hated living in that environment under the same roof as him. Everything about him was abusive. I had never been on my own, and he had me thinking that I was incapable of taking care of myself and my daughter. He had me feeling like I was letting God down and that everything that I was told about my life going down the gutter would be true. The last straw was when he came home after six in the morning. I was up getting dressed for work. I had already dressed my baby and put her cartoons on for her while I finished getting ready. He was sloppy drunk and came in grabbing on me. I kept telling him to leave me alone. He said I was his wife, and if he wanted the p*$$@, he could take it.

He tried throwing me on the sofa, and I came up swinging. He pushed me, I threw a pot at him, and he threw a laundry basket at me, hitting me on my thigh. My leg was killing me, so I tried to call the police, but he took my phone from me. I ended up cutting him on his chin with a knife, running out of the door, and getting my neighbor to call the police for me. I could not believe that this was what had become of my life. The police came, and he was arrested. They smelled the alcohol on him. Because there was no one there to take care of my daughter, and they saw that I was dressed for work, they didn't take me to jail for the cut on his face, but they said that they were going to get child protection involved. I was not willing to endure one more minute of his abuse.

I looked into my sweet baby's face and vowed to protect her at all costs. I thought that I was doing the right thing by marrying her father and making her family whole. I thought that because I sinned, I had to endure that foolishness. But I didn't. I was a sad mess. I called my friend, and she brought me to drop my daughter off at daycare. I resigned from my job, and when I got back home, I put what I could in my car, went back and got my daughter, and drove over five hundred miles back home.

I no longer cared about what anyone had to say about me and my life.

I found my voice, my inner strength. I found my faith again. I understood that my relationship was with God and not with man and that was all that I needed. I slowly put my life back together, and I am doing just fine. My daughter grew up in a wonderful, nurturing household with me. I had the support of my family and friends and am enjoying a happy and fulfilling life. I thought that I would have been missing something, but I was wrong. Parts of me knew I should never have married him and that I could never trust him. My advice to others would be to listen to yourself and not worry about what others would say. People will talk either way, so let them. When something seems off, it is.

When someone shows you who they are, believe them. Don't sign up for foolishness, but if you do, just know that you don't have to remain there.

With God, all things are possible.

Tinya's Bio

Tinya L. Landry, hailing from the vibrant city of New Orleans, LA, is a certified educational leader with nationwide recognition, extending her expertise to all fifty states and the U.S. Virgin Islands.

Her educational journey encompasses an undergraduate degree in Elementary Education, complemented by a graduate degree in Human Behavior. With a career spanning over two decades, Tinya has dedicated herself to the noble profession of education, specializing in nurturing and mentoring both novice and experienced educators, cultivating their abilities to deliver exceptional and captivating lessons to their students, while also empowering them to ascend to leadership roles within the school community.

Tinya's distinct essence is rooted in her role as an encourager, spreading joy, and evoking smiles in those she encounters each day. Her presence infuses any room with laughter and positivity, and she effortlessly connects with people from all walks of life, leaving no room for strangers in her world.

Her genuine warmth and infectious humor serve as powerful assets that consistently contribute to her remarkable success in every endeavor she undertakes.

Above all her accomplishments, Tinya treasures her role as a mother to her two beloved daughters. She cherishes quality time spent with her family and friends, relishing the bonds that enrich her life. With an innate sense of adventure, she embraces the joys of travel and embraces new experiences with open arms.

During her leisure moments, you'll often find her engrossed in books, embodying her commitment to lifelong learning, as she continues to expand her knowledge and horizons.

Contact and Booking Information
Email: tinya.landry@gmail.com

RISING FROM THE ASHES OF THE OUTCRY

By Carlene Nichols

S aturday, March 16 marked the end of my nursing school era. Reggae music and the aroma of Jamaican cuisine filled the air. I wanted to relax with my husband and further celebrate that I am now officially an RN. The tumultuous journey that brought me here was finally over, and it became the catalyst that would change the trajectory of our lives forever. It saved us from homelessness and complete destruction after the outcry.

One evening, my husband planned a movie night with our girls. I got permission from my boss to leave work early, about 9:30 p.m., because I was hoping to catch the tail end of movie night.

As I approached my house, I noticed that the entire house was pitch black with only the TV lights reflecting through the windows. The kids always kept some light on even when watching movies. I instinctively turned my lights off before pulling into the driveway, and I quietly opened the front door.

I was hit with a wave of moaning and groaning sex sounds as I entered. I could cut through the otherwise deafening silence of the house with a knife. I dropped my bags at the door, kicked off my shoes, and sprinted up the stairs. I stood at the top of the stairs panting as I struggled to catch my breath. No one noticed that I entered the room despite my widened mouth and bulging eyes. Mr. ES (the perpetrator) was watching an R-rated movie, "Shottas," with my children.

The scene showed explicit sex in the shower with breasts and butts exposed. Brielle was sitting next to Mr. ES; they were both covered under a blanket. The girls were now eleven and fourteen, and Jacorian was thirteen years old. Everyone's eyes were glued to the TV except for Akheela, seventeen, who covered her head in discomfort. I was in shock and struggled to speak, and I walked over to him quietly in the dark and said, "Have you lost your mind? Why would you watch this movie with the kids? Where is your moral compass?" In patois, he said, "You ah idiot mon, nothing not wrong with the movie."

I felt blood rush to my head, and I screamed at the top of my lungs, "Everyone get up and go to bed NOW!" And no one moved until I screamed expletives. I flipped on the light and grabbed a chair to smash the sixty-inch TV screen. My daughter, Brittney, pushed me back as she wrestled the chair from my grip and said, "Mommy please don't! It's going to explode!" My senses began to return, and I yanked the TV off its stand by the cord

I pointed to Mr. ES, "Idiot get into the room because you are obviously one of the kids." I pushed him, and he staggered into the room before I slammed the door shut. I am usually a calm spirit, and Mr. ES was also shocked by my outrage. I had lost all sense of fear, and I saw his hands shaking and his lips quivering as I screamed at him. Red flags were shooting across my mind, and his questionable behavioral patterns now had more meaning. I stood up on the sofa in my room to ensure that we were eye to eye, and I pointed my finger in his face and said, "Lucifer, where is your moral compass and WHY?"

I reflected on all the preparations he made for movie night, and it was clear that this was malicious and intentional. He simply stood there staring into space. I exited the room, curled up on the floor of my prayer closet, and bawled my eyes out as I prayed for answers.

I had sticky notes on the closet walls with questions asking God to bring me answers and solid evidence for what I was seeing in my spirit. Part of me still wished I was wrong. I prayed for God to give the girls the strength to share verbally what I observed in their behaviors.

On yet another day after coming home early from school, I met Mr. ES (the perpetrator) in our bedroom holding an electric trimmer. He had just shaved Brielle's private area. I immediately reprimanded him. He stated that, "I am a CPS worker, and I know what I am doing." I recognized that it would be futile to call CPS; I would need solid proof for the authorities. He assured me that he knew many investigators at CPS, past girlfriends included, who would vouch for his character. I continued to document his behavior. The next day,

I spoke privately with Brielle, who shockingly stated I was trying to get her dad in trouble. She was manipulated to defend him. I prayed constantly for God to make a way for the girls to speak up, and I was led to the "Surviving R. Kelly" documentary. I obediently showed the film daily at home. Disturbingly, Mr. ES's reaction to the documentary was "Man don't see age, man see meat and some girls want it." On March 21, I had two vivid dreams. One with Mr. ES telling me to sit on a child's penis, and the other with alligators attacking me at St. Catherine High School. My Aunty Precious confirmed that the interpretations meant disgrace.

On May 22, Brielle skipped class, yet Mr. ES insisted on taking her and her sister out to eat. I invited myself. I got on my soapbox and spoke about the same documentary and then about a black head that I saw on Brielle's lip. I took the liberty to talk about herpes, and I explained that "Men will give you money, clothes, and food and use you." For the first time, they both looked at me. Brielle's body language changed, she was less guarded, and she had a perplexed look on her face. "I finally got her attention," I thought.

In a little girl's voice, Brielle said, "Mom can I speak to you privately?" I asked Mr. ES and her sister to leave the room, which he did reluctantly. Brielle asked, "Mom how do you know if someone has a disease." And I said, "Why do you want to know that?" She clarified that her teacher was talking about STDs in class, and she wanted to know more. I explained the disease process and promised to later show her some videos. I knew at that moment that something truly was wrong. I ran to Brittney's room overcome with a feeling of doom and told her "I feel like something terrible is going to happen."

The morning of Saturday, March 23 felt like déjà vu as I awoke to the sound of reggae blasting as the kids did their chores. Unlike March 16, they were both distracted and whispered to

118

each other. Naomi came to my room and said, "Mom, Brielle has something serious to tell you about Dad." I immediately ran to hug her and drove to the corner to speak in privacy.

Brielle burst into tears and melted into my arms and said, "I want to talk about what Dad has been doing to me." She stated that the perpetrator started molesting her just before my wedding, three years prior. "He made me sleep on your couch in the master bedroom when you were at work, and I woke up to him licking my private area. He spread towels and put me on his bed and put his black gross penis in my private area. He also took me to the property barn and put his penis in my butt.

He gives me snacks and clothes when he's done. He sometimes takes us to the Northside home, distracts my siblings with TV while he lays me naked on the bed and licks my vagina, and lies on top of me." I wretched out tears of agony from what I'd heard, and he was doing it to Naomi too. I completely lost it. I sped home immediately. I blasted the horn loudly while screaming Naomi's name. She opened the door, and I yelled, "Grab your shoes and let's go NOW!" Driving madly out of the neighborhood, I wailed at the top of my lungs.

Naomi shared that Mr. ES started molesting her a year later than Brielle, and she documented this in a journal that was used as evidence in court. She said, "He sucked my breasts and pushed his finger into my vagina. He did this on the sofa in your room." She also confirmed receiving money, snacks, and clothes. They both confirmed that he watched sex movies before molesting them. These movies kept coming up on the continue-to-watch list on Netflix. Investigators stated that this was a common practice of molesters.

I called my eldest daughter, Brittney, and sent her home for my safety box of important documents. I immediately shifted into safety mode and notified Mr. ES that I would be working overnight, and the girls would be with me. Brittney rented a hotel room and sent out an urgent text with the hotel address for everyone to meet there. I contacted Mr. Rodgers, an attorney friend, for advice on how to proceed with my report.

I called the police from the hotel, the girls told their stories, and I reported all my observations. I confirmed the discoloration on his penis which was vital evidence that could only be known by those who have seen it. All the pictures of the snacks, clothes, and information I collected on events observed over time became critical as supporting evidence for the case.

On March 24, 2019, I confronted Mr. ES by phone about his behavior, and he did not deny the allegations and confirmed all my warnings. He stated he was not going to anyone's jail and began speaking as if he was suicidal. I sent the police to his location. My eldest son, Barry Bear, advised me to record all conversations with him which was instrumental evidence in court. Using foresight helped us stay one step ahead of him and kept my family safe. All the children were withdrawn from school immediately. We were all interviewed separately by the district attorney at the Child Advocacy Center, and all our stories aligned.

Mr. ES was bailed out by his sister who asked him, "why he took up these dirty CPS children." Unfortunately, this sentiment was echoed by many women within the community. Unfortunately, some of these women were friends. When the news got out, unaware of the wealth of evidence in hand, they circulated many untrue versions of the story. The antagonists in all their stories were myself and my children, with no mention of the perceived protagonist Mr. ES. "She should have known because he started with her when she was fourteen years old," was the popular comment that made me complicit in their minds. A traumatic, repressed wound was ripped open, and after thirty years, I was suddenly aware of my own victimization. The misogynistic rhetoric played for the next four years backing Mr. ES. He posted many pictures of himself on social media, continuing his façade as a trusted CPS worker, coach, and supposedly trusted dad.

Mr. ES's daughter and a friend were sent to do his bidding. The friend showed up at my old residence obviously sent by Mr. ES to retrieve evidence, while on the phone with Mr. ES. He entered the home which was recorded by Barry and used in court. The friend called Mr. ES's daughter and encouraged her to find and befriend us because "Children can change their story." His daughter tried to trick us into trusting her, but her pseudo-supportive act did not work for long. She later posted several TikTok videos condemning me and her dad and later came to defend him in court. Our keen attorneys caught them all in their lies and used their own spoken words and videos against them.

Mr. ES breached every aspect of his protective order. He sent love letters to me from jail, made phone calls, and showed up at church while the children attended youth classes. It climaxed with him showing up at the door of our new apartment, but his ankle monitor had no record of these visits. Mr. Rodgers referred us to Layman's Law Attorney Phillip, who graciously assisted us pro bono. By the end of that week, Mr. ES was re-arrested. His ankle monitor was not charged for twenty-three hours, and Phillip discovered that only the initial hotel we escaped to was programmed into his bracelet as an exclusion zone, leaving our own doorstep vulnerable.

His attorney tried to reduce his bail, and the district attorneys, Alycia and Craig, joined forces with my AVDA-appointed divorce attorney, Kusum. The summary of the events, taped conversations, and all evidence collected were used at his bond hearing. My niece Akheela testified to seeing Mr. ES at the door, and the judge reprimanded him and placed him on house arrest. For the first time, we took a deep breath of relief. Things were still far from easy. His venom even drove the youngest, Naomi, to self-harm and plan to attempt suicide. She had to be hospitalized for mental health treatment.

God provided a therapeutic path for healing and restoration, AVDA referred me to SMOOTH who gave me a makeover. I entered the room full of hate and anger, and Sabrina Greenlee hugged and consoled me. With a heart that spoke from God's own love, she changed the trajectory of my life. I left the event feeling full, empowered, motivated, and ready to tell my story to help others as she helped me.

I began to regain my power. God later blessed me with a new home and new furniture, and I graduated from nursing school with my BSN with president's honors. The girls are now returning to themselves. Naomi now lives with her brother, Travonne Nichols, as she recovers. Brielle was blessed with a bonus foster mother, Yolanda. God separated us to best provide healing. Brielle graduated and is now in college pursuing journalism, and Naomi is now in eleventh grade doing well and plans to pursue law.

Familiar faces showed up to provide support, especially my pastors, Gregg and Linda Crawford, and Aunty Precious, for which I am endlessly grateful. Dr. Calhoun, our beloved counselor, passed away tragically during the process but helped us unpack most of our emotional baggage and created a holistic timeline of events. So, you see despite the inferno, God provided insulation so that the fire could not consume us.

Due to Covid, it took four years for justice to be served. All our stories remained consistent throughout the years. In the case (The State of Texas vs. ES), Detective Lisa Yates led the investigation and did a superb job of collecting evidence.

Under the astute leadership of the district attorneys, Alicia Curtis and Craig Preismyer, we all showed up, testified boldly, and told our stories in power. Justice was served for my girls and me. Justice also flowed downstream to all his unknown victims. Most importantly, I am proud of my heroes, Brielle and Naomi, because their courage ensures that no other little girl will ever experience such trauma from Mr. ES.

Mr. ES (the perpetrator) worked for CPS for over twenty years and was arrested on March 27, 2019. He was convicted by a jury of twelve and sentenced to fifty years in jail. On March 9, 2023, he was charged with continuous sexual abuse of a child. He wanted to be famous and became infamous as this news was broadcast to the whole world.

In retrospect, his behavior that went unchecked created this monster. Mr. ES's behavior started at St. Catherine High School with me as one of his first conquests. While writing my police report, it was the first time I ever unpacked our encounter, and Stockholm syndrome was the label given. It is rumored that he was fired from St. Catherine High School and moved to St. Jago High School. He boasted to my niece how many students he impregnated and all who had abortions. He migrated to America, taught elementary and high school, and worked only in shelters. He designed his life to have boundless access to children, especially the most vulnerable. His group home jobs were mainly girl-populated with allegations of sexual misconduct. It was confirmed that Mr. ES had children with past CPS clients that aged out of care, yet he still had a job there until we reported him.

Lack of accountability in these fields serves the community poorly. Even though he was fired, he was allowed to easily get rehired and repeat the same behavior. This open secret made him believe he was untouchable; he dated people in high places, including CPS investigators to cover his tracks. He frequently verbalized how much he "owned" CPS.

I am now aware of my previous inability to see my own trauma. Born to a schizophrenic mother, I always felt like a reject. This trampled my self-esteem and made me a prime candidate for narcissistic predators like Mr. ES. My culture normalizes these behaviors, so I have never considered myself a victim. Talking to my investigation team was the first safe space to talk about my trauma. I understood that I fell in love with my molester at fourteen years old, while he was twenty-four years of age. Women from my culture turned on me which is the clear reason why we girls don't report molestation and remain traumatized.

The documentary, "Surviving R Kelly," turned out to be the reason the girls spoke up, but it also explained the Stockholm syndrome that I had experienced. I have done my due diligence, and a predator has been taken off the streets. I could not save myself, but I have saved my children and several others who remain voiceless. I am healing, and the grapevine cannot hurt me anymore because I own my story. I will continue to speak to help others free themselves or their children from this vicious cycle and cancer called **pedophilia**!

I will create a safe space where young girls can tell their stories without judgment and thrive in the aftermath, reducing the suicide attempts and mental illness that are the devastating residue of molestation.

Carlene's Bio

Carlene Nichols, RN, BSN, is a compassionate and dedicated registered nurse whose nurturing nature extends beyond her professional achievements into her role as a loving mother and grandmother, affectionately known as "Nana."

In addition to her responsibilities as a foster and adoptive mother, she has poured her heart into providing a stable and caring environment for children in need.

Carlene is the visionary founder of Thriving with Agape, an organization committed to supporting survivors of molestation on their path to recovery and empowerment. A tireless advocate against domestic violence, she leverages her voice to raise awareness and provide crucial support to victims, helping them regain control of their lives.

She also coordinates vital blood drives and serves as a compelling speaker on domestic violence issues, tirelessly working to effect positive change within her community.

Her dedication to making a difference transcends into the realm of literature, where she serves as a contributing writer for Save Yourself women's magazine and co-author of the anthology, *My Walk Past Hell Volume 3: Stories of Survival and Overcoming Domestic Violence.* As a determined advocate for children, her mission is to positively impact young lives, one child at a time. Her unwavering passion for healing and support drives her to help individuals overcome both physical and emotional trauma.

Guided by her profound faith, Carlene embodies the qualities of a true woman of God – love, strength, and resilience – in every facet of her life. Her journey serves as an inspiration to many, and her unwavering commitment to creating positive change continues to touch the lives of countless individuals.

Contact and Booking Information
Email: Carlenenicholsrn56@gmail.com
Facebook: www.facebook.com/carlene.nichols.9

EMPTINESS

By LaVerne Toombs

My life began with emptiness as a child who experienced extreme beatings and harsh words. The verbal and physical abuse continued into my adulthood, causing extremely low self-esteem, seeking out bad relationships, and other physical effects. I don't recall any kind words being said to me, growing up in a rural community in North Louisiana. I never heard the phrase "I love you" or received loving hugs; I only saw affection on television. The form of verbal communication I experienced was daily cursing. My mother told me to pull a limb from the tree to get my butt whipped. Psychological trauma, right? An extension cord or a fan belt from a car engine was also used at times. Whatever the nearest object was she could get her hands on at the time sufficed. She would tie my hands behind my back to prevent me from blocking the object(s). The beatings would be so bad that I would have deep cuts over my entire body because I was stripped down naked to my birthday suit. I guess the Scripture from Proverbs 23:13-14, "Withhold not correction from the child: for if thou beatest him with the rod, he shall not die. Thou shalt beat him with the rod and shalt deliver his soul from hell." Incredibly, I'm still among the living to tell the story. I guess I was spared from HELL. I didn't know about hell, but that was my hell experience. After she whipped me almost to death, she had the nerve to say, "That hurts me as much as it hurts you." What? I know someone can relate to that crazy statement.

I never understood the emptiness in my life, the void from being unloved, unaccepted, and unwanted. Maybe it was because I was adopted and didn't know my biological parents. Perhaps it was from pent-up anger from people I deeply loved suffering from their own issues and insecurities. I dare not say I am perfect, but I know the pain I suffered from the hands and tongue of those I loved.

Proverbs 18:20-21 says, "The tongue has the power of life and death, and those who love it will eat its fruit." Death was spoken into my life from childhood to adulthood, such as being called stupid, ugly, and dumb. My high school peers voted me "Most Likely Not to Succeed." I knew about being bullied before it became a normal narrative in society. I recall being called cat eyes, spotted legs because I was allergic to mosquito bites, and bony because I was very skinny. I had experienced verbal and physical abuse for so long, believing those sentiments was easy. I walked daily with shame, unable or unwilling to openly discuss my feelings.

No one would have understood the hurt and pain I suffered in the community where I was raised. In my generation, especially in a small rural community, people kept silent about abuse, but in their minds, it was normal. You needed to get beaten because you were bad, and you deserved it.

I thought something was seriously wrong with me for many days, weeks, months, and years. How could someone beat you and love you at the same time? Why does a person want to see you succeed in life but beat you down physically and mentally? How is that possible?

Somehow, I became accustomed to the abuse, attempting to create an environment that would be least likely to trigger toxic behavior. I tried to shape myself into a perfectly virtuous child and woman to make a happy space. I continued digging my grave in the name of love and acceptance. One of my common sayings is, "I'm sorry, I won't do it again. I'll do better." I felt the disappointment of wanting to be understood and having a listening ear, but there was none.

Every day, I hoped today would be a good day without being ridiculed or beaten. I had lost my entire sense of self at a young age, and as an adult, I worried if I could make it to the end of the day without suffering verbal or physical abuse. Why can't I smile and laugh like other people do while enjoying life? A dear friend told me, "LaVerne, you need to smile more." For what? I don't have anything to smile about. I'm trying to survive.

Why did the emotional attachment or trauma bond develop a repeated cycle of abuse? The names changed, but the behavior was the same. I left home to avoid a toxic environment and entered other unhealthy environments, and the cycle continued. I had no idea what a healthy relationship looked like.

Why can't I fill this emptiness? Who in their right mind would mistreat me, right? Wrong! I thought a relationship was a privilege, not a chore. Love should be appreciated, not taken for granted. Right?

There are days when I have those flashbacks of the beatings. The worst was when I was eight months pregnant, locked in a closet, and couldn't use the bathroom. Can you imagine being eight months pregnant, unable to urinate, and afraid you might urinate and get beaten for peeing on yourself? I wondered how a person could beat you when you were carrying their child. I remember quietly crying, asking myself, "Am I hated that much? Did I deserve that punishment?" One of the other most horrifying experiences was when I was thrown out of a moving car on the side of a dark road and left there. It was a traumatic experience, creating PTSD.

There were more beatings, but I just named these. I had no life other than trying to avoid verbal and physical abuse. It's hard to believe that I barely spoke and had no eye contact with anyone for years. My life was at work, home, and church. I suffered from anxiety, anger, and self-destructive behaviors.

After fifteen years of my first marriage, I finally got enough courage to leave. I knew it was time to exit from that situation, but I tried to find a way to stay in the marriage because my four children and I had never been alone. And I was a faithful churchgoer being taught that divorce was wrong. I was an emotional ticking time bomb about to explode. No one knew the hell I was suffering inside. Yes, I prayed and fasted. I went to church on Wednesday for Bible study and twice on Sunday.

I didn't know what to ask God for because I thought it was all my fault. Don't get me wrong, I believe in prayer and fasting. At the time, I felt God was punishing me for all my wrongs. I thought I wasn't worthy of God's forgiveness.

I left with $368.00 and the clothes on my back. I moved into an apartment with no furniture and no car. I slept on a dirty mattress I found on the side of the road, which I dragged to the apartment. I applied for food stamps and other services to help me get on my feet. Eventually, I could finally furnish my apartment with used furniture and bought a used red Ford Fiesta, my fantasy Mercedes Benz.

Several months later, I got involved with a gentleman, but that didn't work out. His mother didn't like me. He was a momma's boy. A few months later, seeking to fill the emptiness, I entered another relationship, which was different. He was a good guy, very attentive, loving, and caring. I messed that up because I didn't recognize a healthy relationship. I created drama, forcing him to become what I was trying to avoid. It was like a drug, and I needed drama to function. That's all I knew. After that relationship ended, I took a break and started working on myself. I finally realized I needed help. So, I started reading these self-help books. I didn't know I needed more than self-help books, but I needed therapy due to the years of trauma.

Finally, I sought help after a rock-bottom breakup, which was embarrassing and humiliating because our lives were in the public eye. We were called the power couple. Yeah, right! After two and half years of toxicity and a marriage that lasted less than five months, I traveled down the lane of divorce court. Years later, I discovered that the marriage wasn't legal. This was the breaking point. I called on Jesus for help. HELP ME, PLEASE!

To the outside world, it looked like I had it all together. My professional life was on a roll, but my personal life was an absolute disaster. No one knew my inner pain, suicidal thoughts, and desire to end it all. FUCK it! No one will miss me, not even my children. I sat in my 3700 square foot house with a pool and pool house, living a life of luxury. I had these social gatherings with close friends, and they didn't know the inner pain. It's incredible how well I wore the mask of "I got it together." I only wanted to jump off the nearest bridge or drive into Lake Pontchartrain. Who knew, right?

I decided to take a break from the man addiction, thinking that would fill the emptiness. I need to seek healing. I had reached the breaking point of carrying those heavy burdens for over fifty years. It was time for a transformation. I needed to release the pent-up emotions that prevented my heart and body from embracing my true desires. I needed to understand how to acknowledge and embrace my truth and learn to listen to my inner voice with compassion.

I was blessed to have a therapist who was a believer who shared that harboring ill feelings from past hurts and thoughts of revenge could block the blessings of God in my life. I consciously decided to release the emotional pain of anger, resentment, and bitterness to begin experiencing the freedom that forgiveness brings.

I was given spiritual messages and instructed to block out time for prayer/meditation to connect to my spirituality. In other words, I needed to establish an authentic relationship with God. It caused me to recognize the problems and not make excuses or blame others. I finally stopped being the victim and confessed the hurt I had caused others, such as my adopted mother and children. Most importantly, forgiveness began with me taking responsibility for my actions.

Through therapy, I began self-discovery, and for the first time in my life, I began to value myself deeply and set standards for how I wanted to be treated. I started creating boundaries that safeguarded my well-being and fostered positive connections with myself. This transformation reflected my commitment to nurturing self-love, establishing a foundation for healthier relationships, and experiencing a more fulfilled life.

I finally met a milestone in my life of two and a half years of therapy sessions. I had gone to hell and finally was walking through heaven's gates. I asked the question, "What now?" at my last session, and I was directed to create a statement to remind me not to return to the emptiness. I started "Good Fit," asking is he, this job, or whatever it is a good fit?

I was now fifty-five years old and unemployed after twelve years and eleven months serving as a regional manager due to my boss seeking re-election for the United States Senate. Two weeks later, I was employed as a special assistant to a parish president and later became the chief administrative officer. Guess what? I was dating someone kind, gentle, responsive, and supportive. We went on vacations, to plays and concerts, and experienced fine dining. It was the healthiest relationship ever. We married after two years of dating and a few months of living together. This was it. No more divorce.

This is my life partner; we are going to grow old together. I finally have someone who is going to take the wedding vows seriously. "I take him to be my husband, and he takes me as his wife, to have and to hold from this day forward, for better, for worse, for richer, for poorer, in sickness and health, to love and to cherish, until parted by death. This is my solemn vow."

Don't be too quick to celebrate. I found myself down the road of divorce again after three and a half years of marriage. I allowed the individual to make more withdrawals than deposits in my life. Therefore, I did not know how to close the account. I continued with a negative balance, hoping for reciprocation.

I worked so hard not to return to the toxic behavior but was drowning in defeat. I begged, cried an ocean of tears, and strived to be the best wife. I didn't understand why this was happening to me again. I believed God cursed me due to my disobedience in divorcing my children's father. He's a man of faith and a born-again Christian. By the way, all marriages ended in divorce. Interesting!

Finally, I shared my toxic situation with a trusted friend, asking her to give me wise and godly advice. She asked me, "Why are you still in that situation? Is it because you are concerned about what people will say?" My response was YES! Crazy, right? I've been talked about my entire life. Why am I worried about what people are going to say now? Girl, LaVerne can't keep a man. What number is this divorce? She is going to catch up with Elizabeth Taylor's divorces.

I called my therapist for help. She told me you need to have enough respect for yourself to walk away from an unhealthy situation that no longer serves you, grows you, or brings you peace. If you aren't treated with love and respect, it's not helping you. Understand your worth and stop lowering your standards to fit someone else's standards. Individuals may love you but not know how to love you with their actions. She told me I didn't need any more sessions. I had the essential tools in the toolbox and to open the box and use them. Guess what? She was right.

After the advice from my therapist and spiritual friend, I still tried to make it work. Finally, I realized I needed to walk away from someone who didn't appreciate my value or worth. If I stayed, my soul would continue to be poisoned. I needed to walk away to return to a healthy life. In the end, when you lose an emotional attachment to someone, you realize how ordinary they were to you. It was my love and my energy that made them seem so special.

As painful as it was, I decided to file for divorce. It took me over two years to overcome the disappointment of another failed marriage. I would sit in my house in the dark and scream at the top of my lungs, crying an ocean of tears from the most profound hurt and excruciating pain. There were days when I wanted to end it all because I failed again. The thought of my kids and grandkids kept me encouraged to stay above ground. Prayer and God's guidance helped as well.

Ultimately, I gave too much of myself away and accepted too little in return. I walked away, EMPTY—nothing but a broken heart, disappointment, tears, discouragement, and anger.
I returned to my therapist's advice to open the box and use the tools. I am forever grateful to my therapist, who was God-sent. Unfortunately, my therapist went to be with the Lord during the COVID-19 pandemic. Because of COVID, I couldn't attend the funeral. She will always have a special place in my heart.

One of the tools in the toolbox was a quote, "No matter how great of a woman you are to a man, you will never be good enough if he is not ready." So true. We think the situation will change. We wait, and the results are empty.

My focus is to fall deeply in love with taking care of myself and seeking my God-given purpose, mission, and assignment, staying on the path of continued healing, becoming the best version of myself with patience and compassion, and walking in the footsteps that God has ordered just for me.

It's never too late to start over; being alone is okay. I have closed the chapter of a life of verbal and physical abuse by embracing my peace. I came across this famous quote from Albert Einstein, "Peace is not kept by force but only by understanding." I've learned that peace is obtained in the presence of God and maintained in the revelation that God will fight our battles.

My daily walk is to forgive often, let go, move on, and increase my emotional and spiritual intelligence. I continue to upgrade my boundaries and improve my tolerance so those who hurt me no longer resonate with me. I am enjoying life with my children and grandkids, traveling solo, enjoying life to the fullest, and practicing self-acceptance.

Let me encourage you to take your power back by making choices that are authentic to you by designing your own path. There is light at the end of the tunnel. Psalm 30:5 proclaims, "Weeping may endure for a night, but joy cometh in the morning." Don't give up. Keep the faith. I'm a living witness. Trouble doesn't last always!

LaVerne's Bio

LaVerne Toombs is an accomplished and well-respected communications innovator with a career that spans over two decades. Colleagues, government entities, elected officials, community stakeholders, and prominent organizations have recognized and esteemed her as a capable and dependable grant management and business development expert.

Originally from Northern Louisiana, she has dedicated her life to improving the state and parishes she calls home. She has long been an advocate and champion for equality and civil rights for underserved communities by helping develop and promote inclusivity and awareness for minorities throughout the Greater New Orleans area.

With her magnanimous and infectious personality, LaVerne was recently designated an official TEDx speaker, inspiring broad audiences with her story of being adopted at fourteen.

LaVerne's impressive career includes her titles as the regional manager for former United States Senator Mary Landrieu and the New Orleans Regional Black Chamber of Commerce executive director.

She was also the interim chief administrative officer for community outreach, alum affairs, and public relations at Southern University at New Orleans. She is an adjunct instructor for the popular Grant Writing 101 course at Delgado Community College.

LaVerne founded Right 4 U, LLC, a management and development consulting firm that increases its clients' visibility and impact. She is an award-winning author of *Quick and Easy Steps to Starting a Profitable Home-Based Business*, featured in Essence magazine, and *Tips for Successful Grant Writing*. Both have received many accolades. She also serves on the board of various notable community organizations and has been recognized by several national, state, and local organizations for her passion as a change agent.

In her spare time, she enjoys the company of her four adult children and six loving grandchildren, cycling, and reading good novels.

Contact and Booking Information
Website: ltwrite4u.com
LinkedIn: @lavernetoombs

CLOSING

By Dr. Yolanda J. Henderson

Domestic violence casts a tragic shadow over too many homes and relationships. Yet there is hope. By raising awareness, providing support to victims, enacting smart laws and policies, and promoting respectful attitudes, we can slowly turn the tide against domestic abuse.

Progress starts at the personal level, with each of us examining our own relationships and modeling healthy behaviors. It continues through supporting those in need, whether by lending an ear or giving time and money to aid organizations.

And progress depends on speaking out against violence whenever we encounter it and making clear that assault against loved ones is never acceptable.

The road ahead remains long. But by walking it together, step by step, we can build a society where homes are places of trust, shelter and peace, not fear and harm. Our children deserve no less. If you or someone you know is experiencing domestic violence, please know that support is available. Reach out and know that you do not have to travel this road alone.

God Bless,
Dr. Yolanda J. Henderson

NATIONAL RESOURCES:

- **National Domestic Violence Hotline:**
  1-800-799-SAFE (7233); www.thehotline.org

- **National Coalition Against Domestic Violence:**
  303-839-1852; www.ncadv.org

- **National Dating Abuse Helpline:**
  1-866-331-9474; www.loveisrespect.org

- **National Sexual Assault Hotline:**
  1-800-656-HOPE (4673); www.rainn.org

- **Human Trafficking Resource Center (Polaris):**
  1-800-373-7888; www.polarisproject.org

Made in the USA
Columbia, SC
20 January 2026

77764155R00078